Contemporary English

Second Edition

Book 3

Thomas McNemara

McGraw Hill Contemporary

Acknowledgements

The authors and publisher would like to thank the following people for their help and contribution to the second edition of *Contemporary English:*

First Edition authors: Claudia Rucinski-Hatch, Cheryl Kirchner, Elizabeth Minicz, Mechelle Perrott, Kathryn Powell, Cecelia Ryan, Ardith Loustalet Simons, Kathleen Santopietro Weddel

Series Consultant: **Catherine Porter,** Adult Learning Resource Center, Des Plaines, IL

Grammar Consultant: **Sally Gearhardt,** Santa Rosa Jr. College, Santa Rosa, CA

Reviewers: **Jack Bailey,** Program Coordinator, ESL and Foreign Language, Santa Barbara City College, Santa Barbara, CA; **Kenneth Bretz,** ESL Teacher, Cupertino-Sunnyvale, Cupertino, CA; **Kristine Colina,** Instructor, Crystal Lake Community School. Broward County, FL; **Dianne Gibson Birdsall,** Instructor, College of DuPage, Glen Ellyn, IL; **Ionela Istrate,** Sr. Director, Adult Ed and ESOL, YMCA of Greater Boston, Boston, MA; **Barbara Kremer,** ESOL Director, New Americans Center, Lynn, MA; **Liz Minicz,** Department of Adult Education co-chair, William Rainey Harper College, Palatine, IL; **Paula Orias,** Site Administrator, Piper Community School, Broward County, FL; **Mary Pierce,** Director, Xavier Adult Education Center, New York, NY; **Kathryn Powell,** Instructor, William Rainey Harper College, Palatine, IL; **Annette Ruff-Barker,** Instructor, College of DuPage, Glen Ellyn, IL; **Kristin Sherman,** Instructor, Central Piedmont Community College, Charlotte, NC; **Shirley Taylor,** Project SCALES, West Newton, MA ; **Deborah Thompson,** Instructor, Los Angeles Unified School District, Los Angeles, CA; **Yindra Vanis,** Instructor, Morton College, Cicero, IL

Photo Credits

Page 5: Billy E. Barnes/PhotoEdit; Page 12: Getty Images/Eyewire Collection;
Page 24: © Comstock Images;
Page 29: Michael Newman/PhotoEdit; Page 36: Getty Images/Burke/Triolo Productions;
Page 41: David Young-Wolff/PhotoEdit; Page 48: Getty Images/Donna Day;
Page 53: Michael Newman/PhotoEdit; Page 60: David Young-Wolff/PhotoEdit;
Page 65: Brian Lockett, Goleta Air & Space Museum, www.Air-and-Space.com;
Page 72: David Young-Wolff/PhotoEdit; Page 77: Getty Images/Keith Brofsky;
Page 84: © Kent Knudson/PhotoLink/PhotoDisc/PictureQuest;
Page 89: Logo courtesy of the Better Business Bureau of Chicago and Northern Illinois, Inc.; Page 96: Thinkstock;
Page 101: Felicia Martinez/PhotoEdit, Michael Eacott; Page 108: David Young-Wolff/PhotoEdit;
Page 113: David Young-Wolff/PhotoEdit, Garry Conner/PhotoEdit; Page 120: Getty Images/Eyewire Collection

Executive Editor: Linda Kwil
Senior Editor: Paula Eacott
Art Director: Michael E. Kelly
Production Manager: Genevieve Kelley
Interior Design: WIlliam Seabright and Associates
Interior Illustration: Andrew Lange, Don Petersen, David Sullivan
Cover Illustration: Don Petersen

ISBN: 0-07-253979-8

 **Contemporary**

Send all inquiries to:
McGraw-Hill/Contemporary
One Prudential Plaza
130 E. Randolph St., Suite 400
Chicago, IL 60601
USA

1 2 3 4 5 6 7 8 9 0 QPD/QPD 0 9 8 7 6 5 4 3

Contents

About This Series

Program Components and Philosophy

Contemporary English is a four-level, interactive, topic-based ESL series for adult learners ranging from the high-beginning to the low-advanced level. The series includes

· **Student Books** for classroom use,
· **Workbooks** for independent use at home, in the classroom, or in a lab,
· **Audiocassettes** or **CDs** for individual student, classroom, or lab use,
· **Teacher's Annotated Editions,** with reproducible activity masters and unit progress checks for assessment, and
· **Conversation Cards,** for extra oral pair practice of unit vocabulary and grammar.

These materials have been correlated to the following federal and state standards: the SCANS (Secretary's Commission on Achieving Necessary Skills) Competencies, CASAS Competencies, California Model Standards, the BEST standards, and the Florida LCPs.

Contemporary English empowers students to take charge of their learning and to develop strong communications skills for the real world. Each unit falls under one of the following broad topics: Home and Neighborhood, Family Relations, Employment and Opportunity. In short, the series addresses topics of interest and concern to adult learners.

Unit Structure of the Student Books

Contemporary English provides a controlled and predictable sequence of instruction and activities. Conveniently for teachers, each page of a unit functions as a self-contained mini-lesson. Each unit is divided into two parts, each of which begins with a **Scene** that presents incidents from the lives of newcomers to the United States or aspects of U.S. culture that students encounter regularly. A series of discussion questions proceeds from factual comprehension of the **Scene** to personalization and, in Books 3 and 4, to problem solving.

After each **Scene** comes **Vocabulary** presentation through art or controlled definitions. In Books 3 and 4, students are encouraged to use dictionaries to discover word meanings. Each vocabulary section ends with an exercise that checks basic comprehension of the target words.

Following the vocabulary exercise is a focused listening task that includes pre-listening and post-listening work. **Listening** presents target content and language structures through lively conversations and other samples of natural speech, such as telephone answering-machine messages and transportation announcements.

Throughout *Contemporary English,* grammar structures are first contextualized in the **Scenes** and

listening activities and then presented, practiced, and applied on follow-up **Spotlight** pages. Appearing three times in each unit, the **Spotlight** pages model target structures in contexts related to the unit topic. Special **Spotlight** boxes present the target structures schematically and provide brief, straightforward explanations when necessary. Exercises following the structure presentations allow students to manipulate the structures in meaningful contexts.

Following controlled structure practice on the **Spotlight** pages, listening and speaking skills are developed further in the **Pair Work** activities. Recorded two-person conversations explore the unit topics, structures and vocabulary in natural, colloquial language. Students listen to a conversation and practice it. Students then use this conversation as a model and work in pairs to create their own dialogue. **Spotlight** pages end with a **Your Turn, Talk About It,** and/or **In Your Experience** activity providing communicative application of the new structures.

These last three features occur within the units at specific points, after students have been exposed to structures or ideas in more controlled exercises. **Your Turn** is an oral follow-up to reading, listening, or structure practice. Students can complete the activity alone or in pairs. **Talk About It** is an oral group activity, allowing students to interact within larger groups, applying the vocabulary and structures they have just learned in a personalized conversation. **In Your Experience,** a writing activity that draws on students' prior knowledge and experiences, allows learners to relate the topics to their own lives.

Contemporary English helps students develop their reading skills and become motivated readers of English through **Reading for Real. Reading for Real** includes such real-life documents as a winning job résumé, instructions for office voice mail, biographies of real people, advice from the local police, and ads for cellular phone plans. Follow-up **Talk About It** activities extend and personalize the reading.

In Books 1 and 2, **Organizing Your Ideas** introduces the concept of visual literacy through the use of graphic organizers. T-charts, Venn diagrams, and idea maps help students generate their own ideas on questions related to unit topics. The oral activity at the end of the page encourages students to share and compare their ideas with their classmates.

In Books 3 and 4, **Organizing Your Ideas** is replaced with **Understanding Charts (Tables, Maps, Graphs),** which focuses on information graphics. These activities help students learn to read, interpret, and use information in a graphic format—skills that are crucial in the workplace and in GED preparation. The page concludes with a follow-up activity in which learners develop their own simple graphs or charts and share them with the class.

Problem-solving and critical-thinking skills are developed further in **Issues and Answers,** which contains short letters with views of U.S. life from a variety of perspectives, including those of immigrants and their "cultural advisors." The follow-up activity on this page asks students to use the ideas they generated on the previous page to help the letter-writer solve his or her problem.

Community Involvement provides a channel for students to discover useful inside information about life in the United States. From using the post office to contacting the city council, **Community Involvement** encourages students to go out and explore their neighborhoods. Alternative activities are available for those students who are unable to do research outside of class. No matter which activities are chosen, the information students find will help them adapt to a culture that can be difficult to understand. In-class follow-up activities help students integrate cultural knowledge with their language skills.

At the very end of each unit is **Wrap-Up,** a project requiring students to use a graphic organizer such as a T-chart, a Venn diagram, an idea map, or a timeline to brainstorm, organize ideas, and then use their ideas to present a project to the class. Following **Wrap-Up** is the self-assessment activity **Think About Learning,** a final reflection that asks students to evaluate the quality of their own learning on the major content points, life skills, and language structures in the unit.

Contemporary English is centered around the needs of adult ESOL students: to communicate effectively in English at home, at work, and in their communities. It provides opportunities for adult ESOL students to learn both the language and the culture of the United States.

Icons

Contemporary English uses the following icons throughout the series:

Listening: All Scenes, Listening activities, and Pair Work dialogues are recorded on tape and CD.

Grammar: These exercises may require a variety of language skills, but the main focus is practice of the structure found in the Spotlight box.

Critical Thinking: These exercises require students to perform an activity that requires some analysis or evaluation of information.

Scope and Sequence Book 3

Unit Name/ Number	Vocabulary	Grammar	Language Functions	Graphic Literacy
1 **Machines at Work** *Pages 2-13*	• Office Equipment • Job Training • Office Supplies	• **Review:** Future with *Going To* • **Recycle:** *Could* and *Would* for requests • **Recycle:** Modal *Could* and *Able To* • **Present:** *Because* and *So*	• Ask and answer questions about computer technology at work • Role-play a conversation about office equipment • Describe the new work skills you would like to learn	• Read and analyze a bar graph • Create a bar graph to show how classmates use computers • Create a table showing information on where machines are used
2 **Staying Informed** *Pages 14-25*	• Local Travel • Street Repairs • Local News	• **Review:** Irregular simple past • **Review:** Reflexive pronouns • **Recycle:** *Wh* questions in the past • **Present:** *Suppose To* • **Review:** Simple present	• Discuss recent news in your community • Paraphrase information from a conversation • Interpret a news report using a map	• Read and analyze a pictograph • Create a pictograph about newspaper readership • Create a chart with news and information about your city
3 **Saving Money** *Pages 26-37*	• Telecommunications • Saving Money • Consumer Awareness	• **Recycle:** Ordinal numbers • **Recycle:** Prepositions of location • **Present:** Order of adjectives • **Present:** Present participles as adjectives	• Discuss telephone calling plans • Ask and answer questions on saving money • Talk about a recent purchase	• Read and analyze tables • Create a table showing classmates' use of coupons • Create an idea map on saving money
4 **Trouble at Home** *Pages 38-49*	• Family Relationships • Elderly Care • Emotional Support Agencies	• **Review:** Modals *May, Might* • **Review:** Modals *Should, Ought To, Had Better* • **Recycle:** Direct and indirect objects • **Present:** Commands	• Use commands to role-play a conversation about house rules • Tell ways that people may solve problems at home • Offer advice about services for older adults	• Read and analyze a pie chart • Create a pie chart to show classmates' family infrastructure
5 **Benefits at Work** *Pages 50-61*	• Employee Benefits • Savings • Retirement Planning	• **Review:** Comparative & superlative adjectives • **Review:** *Too* + Adjective • **Recycle:** Adjective order • **Present:** Comparative & superlative adverbs	• Compare job benefits • Role-play a conversation about benefits • Talk about employer-sponsored retirement plans	• Read and analyze a line graph • Create a line graph to show investment growth • Evaluate insurance benefits listed in a chart
6 **Family Heritage** *Pages 62-73*	• Immigration • Culture • Honoring Heritages	• **Recycle:** Future with *Will* • **Present:** Present perfect with *Already, Yet,* and *Just* • **Present:** Present perfect with *Ever* and *Never* • **Present:** Present perfect with *For* and *Since* and simple past	• Share ideas about how you can help your children have pride in your culture • Talk about your favorite native traditions and customs • Ask and answer questions about residency	• Read and analyze a pie chart • Create a pie chart to show which countries classmates are from • Construct an idea map showing how to show pride in your culture
7 **A Healthy Lifestyle** *Pages 74-85*	• Diet • Exercise • Health Insurance	• **Review:** Past continuous • **Recycle:** Past perfect • **Present:** Present perfect continuous • **Present:** Past continuous and the present perfect continuous	• Give advice about reducing stress • Compare traditional insurance to an HMO • Discuss past events that affect the present	• Read and analyze a bar graph • Create a bar graph showing health insurance coverage • Design an idea map that shows how to stay healthy
8 **Consumer Protection** *Pages 86-97*	• Purchases • Returns • Fraud • Consumer Rights	• **Review:** *Have To* and *Should* • **Review:** *Must, Must Not, Don't Have To* • **Recycle:** Commands • **Present:** *Must* for probability	• Tell about a problem you had with a purchase • Role-play a conversation between a clerk and a customer • Talk about options for returning merchandise to a store	• Read and analyze a pie chart • Create a pie chart to show different kinds of consumer problems • Design an idea map showing ways consumers can protect their rights
9 **The Local Park District** *Pages 98-109*	• Community Programs • Recreation • Volunteering	• **Present:** *Used To* • **Present:** Past Perfect • **Present:** Past Perfect Continuous	• Tell where you want to volunteer • Share information about your past experiences • Talk about children's activities	• Read and analyze a bar graph • Create a bar graph to show how class groups volunteered
10 **Body Language** *Pages 110-121*	• Body Language • Interviews • Workplace communication	• **Recycle:** Direct and indirect objects, • **Recycle:** *Like To, Want To, Need To* + Verb • **Present:** Verb + gerunds • **Present:** Verb + infinitives • **Present:** Gerunds and infinitives	• Talk about greetings in your native country • Ask and give advice about preparing for a job interview • Compare formal and informal American body language	• Read and analyze a pie chart • Create a pie chart to show ways people communicate • Construct a T-chart about appropriate body language for an interview

Problem-Solving	Community Involvement	EFF	SCANS	CASAS
• Find places in the community where computer access is free	• Locate and describe places in your community that offer job training	• Learn new skills • Use technology and other work tools	• Foundation skills • Uses technology to complete tasks • Maintains and troubleshoots technology	• **P. 3**, 4.5.1, **P. 5**, 4.4.8, **P. 6**, 4.4.7
• Read a local newspaper to keep informed	• Research English and native language local media options	• Identify and monitor problems, community needs, strengths, and resources • Find, interpret, and analyze diverse sources of information (including own experience)	• Foundation skills • Decision-making	• **P. 15**, 2.3.3, **P. 17**, 2.5.2, **P. 18**, 2.6.3, **P. 19**, 2.2.5, **P. 21**, 3.5.9
• Help resolve a family budget problem through the use of coupons • Read and analyze cell phone calling plans	• Locate stores that have money-saving specials and explain their programs	• Balance and support, work, career, and personal goals	• Foundation skills • Creative thinking • Self-management	• **P. 27**, 1.3.5, **P. 29**, 1.2.2, **P. 31**, 1.2.1, **P. 33**, 1.3.4, **P. 36**, 1.3.3
• Decide who can benefit from meal home delivery services • Discuss ways to solve school problems with your children • Report on services for older adults in your community	• Find information about services in your community that offer support for family issues	• Give and receive support outside immediate family • Form and maintain supportive family relationships	• Foundation skills • Problem-solving • Sociability	• **P. 38**, 7.5.4, **P. 39**, 7.5.6, **P. 41**, 8.3.1, **P. 42**, 8.3.2 **P. 44**, 7.5.3, **P. 45**, 7.5.5
• Advise about benefits of a 401K retirement plan	• Compare benefits offered by local companies where you and your family members work	• Manage work processes and resources	• Foundation skills • Acquires and evaluates information • Responsibility	• **P. 51**, 4.2.4, **P. 52**, 4.2.1, **P. 53**, 4.2.3, **P. 56**, 7.5.1, **P. 58**, 4.2.2
• Suggest ways to help parents teach their children about their heritage	• Use local media resources to report cultural events happening in your community	• Create a vision of future for self and other family members including children and work to achieve it • Pass on values, ethics, and cultural heritage	• Foundation skills • Self-esteem • Works with people of diverse backgrounds	• **P. 63**, 5.1.1, **P. 67**, 2.7.2, **P. 71**, 5.3.6, **P. 72**, 2.6.1
• Find information on temporary COBRA insurance in case you lose a job	• Investigate free or low-cost health clinics in your community	• Provide for physical needs • Pursue personal self-improvement	• Foundation skills • Self-management	• **P. 74**, 3.1.1 **P. 75**, 3.5.9, **P. 76**, 3.5.2, **P. 77**, 7.5.4, **P. 78**, 3.2.3, **P. 84**, 3.1.3
• Tell how the Better Business Bureau can help resolve a purchase problem • Share consumer problems with others and discuss solutions	• Locate consumer advocate groups in your community • Gather specific information on a product before making a purchase	• Communicate so that others understand	• Foundation skills • Organizes and maintains information	• **P. 89**, 1.3.3, **P. 96**, 1.2.2, 1.3.7
• Locate appropriate places for a person who wants to volunteer	• Find out about activities available in your local park district	• Get involved in the community and get others involved • Be a leader within your community	• Foundation skills • Use materials and facilities wisely	• **P. 100**, 0.2.1, **P. 101**, 2.6.1 **P. 102**, 2.5.9, **P. 106**, 2.5.1
• Explain appropriate body language at work to someone from another country	• Observe American body language and examine differences	• Communicate with others inside and outside the organization	• Foundation skills • Works well with others	• **P. 113**, 2.7.3, **P. 112**, 4.4.1, **P. 115**, 0.1.4, **P. 117**, 4.1.5, 4.1.7

Scene 1: Conversation

Read the scene with a partner. Listen to the conversation and practice it together.

Bob is a new employee at Speedy Copies. Sandra is training him.

 Ask your partner the questions below. Share your answers with another pair or the class.

Facts	What are Bob and Sandra doing? What happened?
Feelings	How do you think Bob and Sandra feel? Why do you think so?
And You?	What do you do when you start work? What kinds of things can go wrong?
Comparisons	Do things like this happen at work in your native country?

Your Turn

Now write or tell the story in your own words.

Vocabulary

Look at the pictures and read the words below with a partner. Talk about what the words mean. Use a dictionary if you need it.

burglar alarm

copier

fax machine

fire alarm

microwave oven

security code

smoke detector

to lock

to unlock

to turn on

to turn off

Your Words

_____

_____

to go off = to ring = (machines) to make a loud noise

Exercise 1 Bob works with different machines at Speedy Copies. Match the words in Column A with the sentences about them in Column B. Write the letter.

COLUMN A	COLUMN B
__b__ 1. fire alarm	a. It rings when there is smoke.
_____ 2. burglar alarm	b. It goes off during a fire, and calls the fire department.
_____ 3. smoke detector	c. It makes a loud noise to stop thieves.
_____ 4. security code	d. When you need to use a machine, do this first.
_____ 5. to turn on	e. Do this when you are finished using a machine.
_____ 6. to turn off	f. It stops the alarm from ringing.

Listening

Before You Listen Read about the machines below. What do you think the employees will ask about?

Exercise 2 Listen to the employees at Speedy Copies talk about machines. Circle the letter of the phrase that best describes each problem.

1. The fax machine won't work because
   a. there is no paper.
   b. the paper is jammed.
   c. the machine is not turned on.

2. The computers are down because
   a. the electricity is off.
   b. the phones are not working.
   c. they are not turned on.

3. They need some supplies, so
   a. they're going to call in an order.
   b. they're going to the store.
   c. they're going to fax in an order.

4. She couldn't start her computer, so
   a. she needs to buy a new one.
   b. she needs to check it carefully.
   c. she needs to call a technician.

After You Listen With a partner, compare your answers. Were you right about the employee conversations?

Your Turn

With a partner, talk about one of the machines in your home or workplace. What is it used for? Do you like to use it? Why?

SPOTLIGHT on *Because* and *So*

Cause	Effect
The copy machine is jammed,	**so** I can't make my copies.
Sergio had to work on Saturday,	**so** he missed the party.

Effect	Cause
I can't make my copies	**because** the copy machine is jammed.
Sergio missed the party	**because** he had to work on Saturday.

The copy machine is jammed, **so** I can't make my copies.
Sergio missed the party **because** he had to work late.
Because he had to work late, Sergio missed the party.

Use a comma before **so**. When the clause with **because** comes first, use a comma. If the **because** clause is second, don't use a comma.

 Exercise 3 Read about things that happened to people at Speedy Copies. Match the sentence beginning in Column A with sentence ending in Column B. Write the letter.

<u>COLUMN A</u>

__c__ 1. She didn't punch in the security code,

_____ 2. My company closed,

_____ 3. I can't make the copies

_____ 4. I needed to be at work at 6:00 A.M.,

_____ 5. At work today the fire alarm went off

_____ 6. She installed a burglar alarm

<u>COLUMN B</u>

a. so I need to find a new job.

b. because there was a small fire in the kitchen.

c. so the burglar alarm went off.

d. so I left for work early.

e. because the copier isn't working.

f. because she was worried about someone robbing the store.

Exercise 4 In your notebook, complete these sentences with <u>so</u> or <u>because</u> and another sentence. Write about yourself. Use commas when necessary.

I was late for work . . .   The copier broke . . .   I didn't turn on the microwave oven . . .
. . . I couldn't make the copies . . . we bought a new smoke detector.

 ## Pair Work

Listen to the conversation between Mr. Curtiss and Sandra. Then practice it with a partner.

Mr. Curtiss: Did you send the fax?

Sandra: No, I couldn't send it because the fax machine is broken.

Mr. Curtiss: What are you going to do?

Sandra: Well, there is a fax machine in the customer service department, so I could send it from there.

Mr. Curtiss: That's a good idea.

In Your Experience

In your notebook, start two sentences about machines at your workplace. Use the sentence starters from Exercise 4 to help you. Then exchange sentences with a partner. Use **so** and **because** and another sentence to complete your partner's sentences. Use commas when necessary. Share your completed sentences with another pair or with the class.

Reading for Real

Bob uses computers every day, but he wants to learn more about them. There are many sources of computer training in his community. Johnson City Community College has some one-day classes in using computers.

Computer Training

These one-day classes give adults fast, practical computer training for work or school. Each class is offered twice, once on Saturday, and once on Tuesday. Learners may sign up for any or all of the classes and do not need to take them in order.

Computers 1: Introduction to Personal Computers
Find out how to connect your computer and start it.
Find out how to perform simple repairs on your computer.
Saturday, November 16, 9:00 A.M. to 1:00 P.M.
Tuesday, November 19, 6:00 A.M. to 10:00 P.M.
Fee: $12, for computer disks and supplies

Computers 2: Using a Computer at Work
Learn how to use a computer to type letters and other simple documents.
Saturday, November 23, 9:00 A.M. to 1:00 P.M.
Tuesday, November 6:00 A.M. to 10:00 P.M.
Fee: $20, for computer disks, paper, and supplies

Computers 3: Internet Basics
In this class, you will learn to use the Internet to find information and to send email.
Saturday, November 30, 9:00 A.M. to 1:00 P.M.
Tuesday, December 3, 6:00 A.M. to 10:00 P.M.
Fee: $15, for computer disks and supplies

 Exercise 5 Bob's friends want to take computer classes too. Which class should each one take? Read the brochure again. Write <u>Computers 1</u>, <u>Computers 2</u>, or <u>Computers 3</u> on the lines.

1. Carla has an old computer. She wants to find out how to fix it when it breaks.

   _____

2. Mustafa wants to send e-mail to his relatives in Morocco. _____
3. Frank needs to use a computer to write letters and forms at work.

   _____

4. Rosa is a teacher's aide. She wants to learn about the Internet so she can help the children use it. _____
5. Joe needs to take the least expensive class. _____
6. Kristina wants to know how to connect her new computer. _____

 ## Talk About It

In a group, ask and answer these questions.
How can computer knowledge help you at work?
Which computer training class will help you at work?

Scene 2: Conversation

Read the scene with a partner. Listen to the conversation and practice it together.

Bob is busy working at the copy shop.

 Ask your partner the questions below. Share your answers with another pair or the class.

Facts	What is Bob doing? What's wrong with the copier?
Feelings	How does Bob feel? How do you know?
And You?	What do you do when machines aren't working at your job?
Comparisons	Who fixes machines at workplaces in your native country, you or a repair person?

Your Turn

Now write or tell the story in your own words.

Vocabulary

Look at the pictures and read the words below with a partner. Talk about what the words mean. Use a dictionary if you need it.

battery   button   computer disk   cord   lever

jammed   to fix   to push

Exercise 6 Bob is ordering supplies for the copy shop. Complete the sentences. Write the correct word on the line. Use the words above to help you.

1. My radio isn't working. It needs a new _____.

2. Push the _____ to turn on the fax machine.

3. Copy the file to _____, then you can take it to another computer.

4. Sometimes paper becomes _____ in the computer printer.

5. In an emergency, _____ the door open.

Listening

Before You Listen Look at the pictures below. Name the machines. Which supplies do you use with these machines?

Exercise 7 Listen to the conversations at Speedy Copies. Write the name of the machine on the line. Then circle the supplies that people need.

1. _____   cord   battery   computer disk
2. _____   button   battery   computer disk
3. _____   paper   lever   cord
4. _____   paper   lever   cord
5. _____   button   lever   battery

After You Listen With a partner, compare your answers. Were you right about the supplies?

Talk About It

In a group, ask and answer these questions. Where do people keep supplies at work or at home? What happens if they run out of something important, such as batteries for smoke detectors?

I'm **going to copy** these letters.
You're **going to copy** these letters.
He's **going to use** the computer.
She's **going to use** the computer.
It's **going to need** a new battery.
We're **going to send** a fax.
They're **going to send** a fax.

I'm not **going to copy** these letters.
You're not **going to copy** these letters.
He's not **going to use** the computer.
She's not **going to use** the computer.
It's not **going to need** a new battery.
We're not **going to send** a fax.
They're not **going to send** a fax.

Questions

Am I **going to fix** the copier?

Are you **going to copy** these letters?

Is she **going to buy** new batteries?

Short Answers

Yes, you **are**./No, you **aren't**.

Yes, we **are**./No, we **aren't**.

Yes, she **is**./No, she **isn't**.

Use **be + going to + verb** to talk about future events that you expect to happen soon.

Exercise 8 Read about what Bob and Sandra are doing at work. Complete the sentences. Use <u>be</u> + <u>going to</u> and the verbs below.

1. Bob ___'s going to make___ (**make**) copies.

2. The copier is jammed. They _____ (**fix**) the copier.

3. They _____ (**work**) together.

4. Sandra _____ (**tell**) Bob how to fix the copier.

5. She _____ (**not open**) the door of the copier. Bob will open it.

6. He _____ (**push**) a button and turn a lever.

7. Then he _____ (**take out**) the jammed paper.

8. Bob _____ (**not tear**) the paper.

9. Last, he _____ (**close**) the door.

10. Sandra _____ (**not call**) the copier repair man.

Exercise 9 In your notebook, write sentences about what you are going to do at work or at home tomorrow. Write sentences about what you are not going to do tomorrow too. For example, write "I'm going to fix the old computer. I'm not going to buy a new computer."

 Talk About It

In a group, take turns asking and answering questions about what you are going to do tomorrow. Use the sentences from Exercise 9 to help you. How many people are going to do the same things?

SPOTLIGHT on Review Future with *Will*

I'll **help** Bob fix the copier.

You'll **help** Bob fix the copier.

He'll **find** some paper.

She'll **find** some paper.

It'll **go off** if there's a thief.

We'll **need** a new disk.

They'll **need** a new disk.

I **won't help** Bob fix the copier.

You **won't help** Bob fix the copier.

He **won't find** some paper.

She **won't find** some paper.

It **won't go** off if there's a thief.

We **won't need** a new disk.

They **won't need** a new disk.

Will you **make** these copies?

Will they **call** the copier repair service?

Use **will + verb** to talk about promises and plans.

Yes, I **will.** / No, I **won't.**

Yes, they **will.** / No, they **won't.**

Exercise 10 Complete the sentences about things Bob and Sandra plan to do. Use <u>will</u> or <u>will not</u> and the verbs below.

1. She _____'ll help_____ (**help**) Bob repair the copier.

2. She _____ (**show**) Bob how to open and close the shop.

3. Bob _____ (**learn**) to use the computer.

4. He _____ (**buy**) supplies for the shop.

5. She _____ (**become**) assistant manager in a year.

6. She _____ (**not hire**) a new employee.

7. He _____ (**not train**) the new employee.

8. They _____ (**get**) raises next year.

Exercise 11 In your notebook, write sentences about things you plan to do in the next 5 years. Use future with <u>will</u>. For example, write "In five years I will be a manager. I won't have to work nights."

Pair Work

Listen to the conversation between Bob and Sandra. Then practice it with a partner.

Sandra: At this job you'll need to use the computer every day.

Bob: What will I have to use it for?

Sandra: You'll order a lot of supplies on the computer.

Bob: What else will I do with it?

Sandra: You could use it to type memos to the employees.

Talk About It

In a group, ask and answer these questions. What are your plans for the next five years? What will happen to you? Who has the most interesting plans in your group? Share your answers with the class.

Understanding Bar Graphs

Bob saw this graph about computers in the company newsletter. A government study showed the percentage of U.S. homes that had computers from 1984 to 2000.

With a partner, look over the graph. Did the number of homes with computers go up or down?

U.S. Homes with Computers 1984–2000

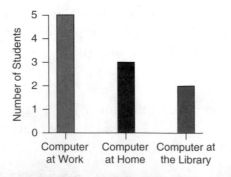

(Bar graph: Percentage of U.S. Households with Computers vs. Years)

- 1984: about 8%
- 1989: about 15%
- 1993: about 22%
- 1998: about 42%
- 2000: about 51%

Exercise 12 Bob isn't sure he understands the information in the graph. In your notebook, answer his questions about the graph.

1. Who found this information?
2. Is the information about the world or only the United States?
3. Is the information about the number of computers or the cost of computers?
4. What percentage of homes had computers in 1984?
5. When did 22 percent of homes have computers?
6. What percentage of homes had computers in 2000?
7. Why is the number of computers growing so rapidly?
8. What percentage of homes do you think will have computers in 2010?

Talk About It

In a group, find out how many learners use a computer at work, at home, and at the library. Write the answers you hear. Next, make a bar graph to show the results. Follow the example below. Use information from all the graphs to create a class graph.

(Bar graph: Number of Students)

- Computer at Work: 5
- Computer at Home: 3
- Computer at the Library: 2

Issues and Answers

Bob's co-worker, Phil, wrote to Ms. Moneybags. Read the letter and Ms. Moneybags' advice. Then talk with other students about the advice. Do you agree? What other advice can you give?

Ask Ms. Moneybags

DEAR MS. MONEYBAGS,

I have a problem at work. My boss says that I can't get a promotion because I don't have computer skills. I want to learn to type letters and to use the Internet. However, computers are very expensive. How am I going to learn computer skills with no computer?

—WORRIED

DEAR WORRIED,

There are many ways to learn computer skills. Computers are inexpensive now. You can also find used computers. Many stores sell used computers for a lot less money than new ones. Always be careful when you buy a used computer. Check it carefully, and have a friend check it too. You are also able to use computers at public libraries, usually for free. You can use these computers while you look for one to buy.

Good luck,
—MS. MONEYBAGS

Your Turn

Worried needs to find an inexpensive computer. Help Worried solve his problem.

Step 1: With a partner, list places in your community that have computers. List computer stores and places where people can use computers for free. Use the telephone directory or a newspaper to help you.

Step 2: Tell Worried where to go to use computers for free. Then use newspaper ads to find a computer that is not very expensive.

Step 3: Share the information you found with the class.

Community Involvement

With the right skills, people can get a new job or a promotion. Employers want their workers to have the best skills for the job, so many businesses offer training classes.

People can also take training classes at job centers and community colleges to learn how to use the machines at their jobs.

Your Turn

What new work skills do you want to learn? List three office machines you would like to learn how to use at your job. Share your list with a partner. Why do you want to learn about these machines? Will they help you get a better job?

Community Action

Step 1: Talk about your list of skills with your coworkers or friends. Are there any skills they want to add to the list? Write them down.

I want to learn _____

_____

_____

My friends and coworkers want to learn _____

_____

Step 2: Make an appointment to talk with your supervisor before or after work. Or talk with a job counselor. Tell your supervisor or counselor the skills you want to learn from Step 1. For example, ask "Where can I get training to learn how to use the fax machine and printer?" Write down the answers to your questions.

 ## Talk About It

In a group, talk about the training you found. What training is offered in your community? Which training class do you want to take? Why?

Wrap Up

Bob and Sandra use machines every day—either at work or at home. In a group, talk about the machines below. Where can you find them? Write the words in the columns. Add three machines of your own. Some machines are used in more than one place.

answering machine	fax machine	telephone
burglar alarm	fire alarm	TV
cell phone	smoke detector	VCR
computer	tape player	

Home	Work	School	Library
telephone	telephone	telephone	telephone

With a partner, talk about machines at work or at home. Use **so, because, be + going to,** and **will.** Use words from this unit. For example:

A: What machines do you use at work?

B: I use a telephone and an answering machine. I'm going to get a fax machine

A: What do you use the telephone for?

B: Well, customers call in with orders. I also call customers if I have questions.

A: Why do you need an answering machine?

B: Because I have a lot of meetings. The answering machine takes a message when I am not there.

Practice your conversation. Then share it with the class.

Think About Learning

Check (✔) to show your learning in this unit. Then write one more thing you learned.

SKILLS / STRUCTURES	PAGE	EASY ☺	SO-SO 😐	DIFFICULT ☹
Understand instructions for a machine	2, 6			
Understand conversations about machines	3, 7			
Talk about problems with machines	3			
Use **because** and **so**	4			
Read a brochure about computer classes	5			
Use **be + going to**	8			
Use **will** for future plans	9			
Read and create a bar graph to express ideas	10			
Learn about technical training in your community	12			

Scene 1: Conversation

Read the scene with a partner. Listen to the conversation and practice it together.

Andrea needs to go to 4250 Water Street. Sue just heard that Water Street is closed.

 Ask your partner the questions below. Then share your answers with another pair or the class.

Facts	What street is closed? Why?
Feelings	How do you think Andrea feels about the news? Why do you think so?
And You	How do you find out news and information?
Comparisons	Do streets close for repairs in your city or town?

Your Turn

Now write or tell the story in your own words.

Vocabulary

Look at the pictures and read the words below with a partner. Talk about what the words mean. Use a dictionary if you need it.

| major blizzard | minor snowstorm | delivery | detour | downtown | repairs |

recent = happened only a short time ago
to find out = to learn, discover
to stay informed = to always know what is happening

Your Words

_____

_____

Exercise 1 Andrea heard a news report on the radio. Complete the sentences. Write the correct word on the line. Use the words above to help you.

1. Park Avenue is closed for repairs. Take a _____ on River Road.

2. There was a terrible _____ last night. Almost one foot of snow fell.

3. I listen to the radio every morning so I can _____.

4. I need to take this _____*delivery*_____ of clean clothes to 1600 Oak Street.

5. Here's a _____ map of the repairs downtown. It was in the newspaper today.

Listening

Before You Listen Read the questions about what is happening in the city. What do you think the radio news will talk about?

Exercise 2 Listen to what Andrea heard on the radio. Circle the letter of the phrase that best answers each question.

1. What happened in the city last night?
   a. a major blizzard
   b. a minor snowstorm
   c. heavy rain

2. What will the weather be tonight?
   a. a major blizzard
   b. a minor snowstorm
   c. heavy rain

3. When did the repairs on Water Street begin?
   a. Monday morning
   b. Tuesday morning
   c. Wednesday morning

4. What happened at the public library?
   a. a major fire
   b. a minor fire
   c. a blizzard

After You Listen With a partner, compare your answers. Were you right about the events Andrea heard on the radio?

Your Turn

With a partner, talk about recent news in your city or town. Were there fires? accidents? bad weather? What happened? When did it happen?

SPOTLIGHT on Review Irregular Past

Many English verbs have irregular past tense forms.

I **heard** the news about the blizzard.
You **took** a detour on Lake Street.
He **ran** away from the police.

We **saw** the news on TV.
She **bought** a newspaper.
They **built** a new park downtown.

In affirmative sentences, use the irregular past tense form.

When **did** you **buy** the food?   **Did** you **buy** a newspaper?   I **didn't buy** a newspaper.

In questions and negatives, use **did** or **did not** and the base form of the verb.

Exercise 3 Sue is talking to Andrea about some recent news. Complete the sentences. Write irregular past verbs on the line.

Sue: (1) _____Did_____ you **hear** the news? The city
          _____ (2) **begin** a new building project last week.

Andrea: Yes, my brother _____ (3) **tell** me. They're going to build a
          new library in our neighborhood, right?

Sue: That's right. I _____ (4) **see** the plans for the library last
          week in the newspaper.

Andrea: That's great. I _____ (5) **not go** to the old library downtown.

Sue: Yes, the downtown library ___hasn't___ (6) **not have** a lot of
          space for community activities.

Exercise 4 What did you do yesterday? In your notebook, write four or five sentences about what you did yesterday. Write about what you didn't do, too. For example, write "Yesterday, I didn't drive downtown. I knew that Water Street was closed. Traffic was stopped. I went home because there was no parking."

Pair Work

Listen to the conversation between Andrea and her husband. Then practice it with a partner.

Andrea: Did you read the newspaper this morning?
Brad: No, I didn't. What happened?
Andrea: Well, there was a major train accident north of town. More than fifty people
          went to the hospital.
Brad: That's terrible. When did you read about the accident?
Andrea: I read the newspaper on the train.

In Your Experience

In a group, talk about what you did yesterday. Share your sentences from Exercise 4. Use everyone's information to write a paragraph about what people in your group did yesterday.

Reading for Real

Andrea reads the *Southtown News*. It has news and information for people on the south side of the city. This article is about the Park Street Neighborhood Association.

Park Street Neighborhood Association Makes a Difference

The Park Street Neighborhood Association recently began two projects. First, the association started a neighborhood clean-up program.

Every Sunday at 5:00 P.M., the neighbors begin cleaning Park Street from one end to the other. According to the group's president, Elsa Santos, said, "The first Sunday, only eleven people came, but we picked up over seven big bags of trash from the sidewalk and street. The next weekend, twenty people came, and filled eight big trash bags. Now the neighborhood really looks great!"

The neighbors on Park Street also began a Neighborhood Watch Program to look for problems in the neighborhood and to call the police if necessary. According to neighbors, the watch has already helped.

Miss Mildred Werner, 75, a retired teacher, said, "In the past, I felt afraid at night. Now I know that my neighbors are watching for trouble." According to police, there are fewer problems on Park Street.

Police Officer Frank Loyola said, "Calls to 911 went down last month. Criminals know that the people on Park Street are watching, so they stay away."

The neighborhood association has other plans too. "We want to start an after-school club for children. And we want to have a picnic for everyone in the neighborhood" said Elsa Santos.

criminal

Exercise 5 Andrea learned about her neighborhood association in the newspaper. Are the sentences correct? Read the article again. Write <u>yes</u> or <u>no</u> on the line.

_____ 1. The Southtown News cleaned Park Street.

_____ 2. The clean-up helped the neighborhood.

_____ 3. The police started a neighborhood watch on Park Street.

_____ 4. Criminals don't go to Park Street because of the neighborhood watch.

_____ 5. The neighborhood association wants to have a picnic.

_____ 6. The neighborhood association started an after-school club for children last year.

Talk About It

In a group, ask and answer these questions. How can you stay informed about your neighborhood? How could a neighborhood association help your neighborhood? Do people in your neighborhood work to keep it clean?

Read the scene with a partner. Listen to the conversation and practice it together.

Andrea is coming back from her delivery on Water Street. It took a long time.

 Ask your partner the questions below. Share your answers with another pair or the class.

Facts	What did Andrea find out? Where did she find the information?
Feelings	How do you think Sue feels about Andrea's information? Why do you think so?
And You?	Do you read newspapers? How often?
Comparisons	How do people find out news and information in your city or town?

Your Turn

Now write or tell the story in your own words.

Vocabulary

Look at the pictures and read the words below with a partner. Talk about what the words mean. Use a dictionary if you need it.

special = used for only one reason or occasion

| article | a copy (of the newspaper) | parking lot | traffic | to be back = to return | to park |

Exercise 6 In the city, there is always something happening that Sue needs to know. Complete the sentences. Write the correct word on the line. Use the words above to help you.

1. Don't take Lake Street this morning. It has very heavy ___traffic___.
2. It's hard to drive downtown. People may need to use a ___special___ bus because of the construction.
3. According to a newspaper ___article___, the city will build a new library.
4. Many people ___parking___ their cars and take the train to work.
5. Sue decided to read ___copy___ of the newspaper every day.
6. Some people park in a ___parking lot___ near their work.

 # Listening

Before You Listen With a partner, look at the map. What are the names of the streets? What other places are on the map?

Exercise 7 Listen to the news report. Write <u>repairs begin</u> and <u>repairs end</u> on the map. Write <u>P</u> for parking and <u>B</u> for bus stop on the map.

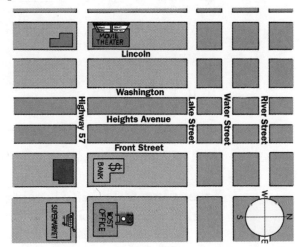

After You Listen With a partner, compare your answers. Did you correctly put the information on the map?

 Your Turn

With a partner, look at the map again. Ask and answer these questions. You need to go to the corner of Water Street and Lincoln Boulevard. Can you drive there, or should you park and take the bus? If you take the bus, which bus stop should you use?

SPOTLIGHT on *Supposed To*

> You're not supposed to walk dogs in this park.

I **am supposed to** deliver these clothes to 4250 Water Street.
You **are supposed to** listen to the news to stay informed.
He **is supposed to** take the detour.
She **is supposed to** deliver these clothes to 4250 Water Street.

We **are not supposed to** drive on Water Street.
They **are not supposed to** take the detour.

Use **supposed to** to talk about things you should and should not do.

The repairs **are supposed to** be finished in May.

Use **supposed to** in the present to talk about actions that we think will be completed in the future.

You **were supposed to** find out about the repairs yesterday.
She **wasn't supposed to** work yesterday.

Use **supposed to** in the past for things that were expected to happen, but didn't, or that were not expected, but did happen.

Exercise 8 Andrea and Sue learned a lot of information from the newspaper article. Complete the sentences. Use the correct form of **be** + **supposed to** on the line.

1. The city _____ is supposed to _____ open a new parking lot.

2. People **(not)** _____ park in the lots on Water Street.

3. Delivery drivers _____ load and unload on Lake Street.

4. Water Street _____ be finished in January.

5. When Water Street is finished it _____ be very nice.

6. It _is supposed to_ have more parking.

7. There _are supposed to_ be better bus stops.

8. The sidewalks _are supposed to_ wider.

Exercise 9 The city is going to build a new park in your neighborhood, and your neighborhood association is in charge of the project. In your notebook, write five sentences about the project. Write rules for the park too. Use **supposed to**. For example, write "The park is supposed to have a picnic area. People aren't supposed to walk dogs in the new park."

Talk About It

In a group, talk about news in your city or town. Tell what the city is supposed to do in the future. Talk about repairs, new schools, and so on. Use **supposed to**. For example, say, "The city is supposed to finish work on the corner of Riverside Drive and Highway 57."

SPOTLIGHT on Review Reflexive Pronouns

I hurt **myself.**
You injured **yourself.**
He cut **himself.**
She burned **herself.**
It hurt **itself.**

We saw **ourselves** on TV.
They hurt **themselves.**

Use reflexive pronouns when the person who did the action and received the action are the same.

I bought **myself** a newspaper.
Also use reflexive pronouns for emphasis.

Exercise 10 Andrea and Sue heard many things about their neighborhood. Write the correct reflexive pronoun on the line.

1. A woman slipped on the floor and hurt _____herself_____.

2. We saw _____ on the news on TV last night!

3. Three people hurt _____themselves_____ in an accident on Front Street.

4. I hope you and Max enjoy _____yourself_____ at the movies.

5. You need a hammer. Go to the garage and get _____ a hammer.

6. The computer turned _____itself_____ off automatically.

Exercise 11 Sue heard about a fire on the news. Read the interview. Complete the sentences. Write the correct reflexive pronoun on the line.

There was a fire at the computer factory where I work. I saw the fire and called the fire

department **(1)** _____myself_____. A woman hurt **(2)** _____herself_____

while she was leaving the building. Two men slipped on the stairs and cut

(3) _____themselves_____ pretty badly. A firefighter burned

(4) _____himself_____ while fighting the fire. Luckily, I wasn't hurt

(5) _____myself_____.

Pair Work

Listen to the conversation between Andrea and her father. Then practice it with a partner.

Andrea: Have you ever hurt yourself at work?

Art: No. I was in an accident at work, but I didn't hurt myself. Some boxes fell off a high shelf. Luckily, they were empty. A friend of mine hurt herself at work. She cut herself with a knife.

Andrea: Some knives are so sharp, they can cut all by themselves.

In Your Experience

In your notebook, write a paragraph about you or someone you know accidentally hurting themselves. Use reflexive pronouns. What happened? When did it happen? What did you do? Share your paragraph with the class.

Understanding Pictographs

Andrea and Sue now read the paper every day. The Newspaper Association of America gathered some information about newspapers and newspaper readers.

With a partner, look over the information and the graph. Do more people read newspapers during the week, or on weekends?

> **a v e r a g e**
>
> **normal, usual**

· There are about 1,480 newspapers in the United States.
· On average, about two people read each copy of a newspaper.
· On an average day, 55 percent of people read a newspaper.

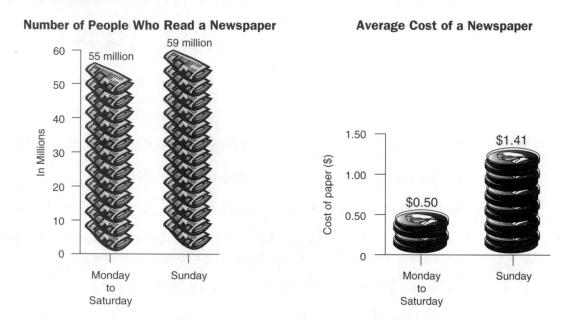

Exercise 12 When Sue started reading the newspaper, she was surprised at how many other people also read the newspaper. In your notebook, answer the following questions.

1. It's Wednesday. How much does an average newspaper cost?
2. It's Sunday. How many people read a newspaper?
3. What percentage of people read a newspaper on an average day?
4. On an average day, what percent of people don't read a newspaper?
5. On average, how many people read a copy of a newspaper?
6. How many newspapers are there in the United States?
7. It's Thursday. How many people read a newspaper?
8. Why is a newspaper more expensive on Sunday?

Talk About It

In a group, find out how many people read a newspaper in English or another language at least once a week. Write the answers you hear. Next, make a pictograph to show the results. Follow the example above. Use information from all the graphs to create a class graph.

Issues and Answers

A new employee at the dry cleaner's wrote to Abdul and Anita. Read the letter and Abdul's advice. Then talk with other students about the advice. Do you agree? What other advice can you give?

Ask Abdul and Anita

DEAR ABDUL AND ANITA,

I just moved to my town. I feel very confused. For example, last weekend there was a big music festival here. But I did not know about it. I found out on Monday at work. Then it was too late for me to go. Yesterday, I took my kids to school to sign up for classes in August. The secretary at the school told me that I am supposed to register my kids next month. Then today, I wanted to go to the post office. But when I got to the post office, I found out that the post office was closed for a holiday. How do I stay informed about what is happening in my new town?

—CONFUSED

DEAR CONFUSED,

There is a simple answer to your problem: Buy a newspaper. A newspaper has all the most important information on what is happening in your town and also what is happening in the country and the world. Newspapers have information on music festivals. Newspapers also have information about holidays. Newspaper ads can help you shop, find a house or an apartment, or get a job. All of this information is very inexpensive too. In most cities, a daily newspaper costs only about 50 cents. So, get a newspaper and keep yourself informed.

Happy reading!

—ABDUL

Your Turn

Confused should start reading a newspaper so she can stay informed. Help Confused by finding out the kinds of information she can read about in a newspaper.

Step 1: With your group, look over the newspaper. Decide which sections might help Confused stay informed.

Step 2: Find two articles about traffic or street repairs in your town in the newspaper. Make a list of the places where there could be traffic problems.

Step 3: Share your list with the class. Also tell the class the names of the sections where you found the articles with the information.

Community Involvement

It's important to stay informed about your community. You can learn about new jobs. You can learn about concerts and festivals. You can find out about sales at the supermarket. There are many ways to find out news and information. You can read a newspaper or a magazine. The radio and TV have news too.

Your Turn

With a partner, talk about newspapers and television news in your native country. Did you read the newspaper? Did you watch the news on television? Why or why not? How are the newspapers and news programs different from newspapers and television news in the United States?

Community Action

Step 1: With a partner, make a list of things you both want to know about your community. Include things such as current events, festivals, and public programs. Put the most important things at the top of the list.

Step 2: With your partner, choose two sources of information in your community that will tell you what you want to know. You can list newspapers, radio, and TV stations in English or in other languages. Find the answers to these questions:
- What is the name of the newspaper?
- What language is it?
- How much does it cost?
- Where can I buy it?
- What is the name of the radio or TV station?
- What language is it?
- What time is the news on?

Talk About It

In a group, talk about sources of information you found. Which ones answered your questions? Which ones will you read or listen to in the future? Why? Create a group list of good information sources for your community. Share your list with the class.

Wrap Up

Now Andrea and Sue read the newspaper every day to find out what is happening in their city. Work with a partner. Make a chart like the one below in your notebook. Complete the chart with news and information about your city. Write about things that happened and things that didn't happen. Write about things the city is supposed to do and not supposed to do too.

Happened	Didn't Happen
Supposed To Do	Not Supposed To Do

With a partner, role-play a newscast about your community. Each person is a news anchor. Use the information in your charts to tell what happened or what is supposed to happen in your town. Use irregular simple past, **supposed to,** and reflexive pronouns. Use words from this unit. For example:

A: Good morning, everyone. At the top of the news, a major blizzard hit last night. The city is supposed to clear the streets of snow, but so far most streets are still closed.

B: There was an accident during the storm. A truck hit a car on Highway 57. The truck driver did not hurt himself, but the woman in the car went to the hospital. The city says that people aren't supposed to drive until noon today so that workers can clear the roads.

Practice your role-play. Then share it with the class.

Think About Learning

Check (✔) to show your learning in this unit. Then write one more thing you learned.

SKILLS / STRUCTURES	PAGE	EASY ☺	SO-SO 😐	DIFFICULT ☹
Talk about news in your community	15, 20			
Understand news broadcasts	15, 19			
Use irregular verbs in simple past	16			
Read and understand news stories in a newspaper	17, 23			
Use **supposed to**	20			
Use reflexive pronouns	21			
Read and create a pictograph to express information	22			
Read about and solve problems with a group	23			
Learn about sources of information in your community	18, 24			

Scene 1: Conversation

Read the scene with a partner. Listen to the conversation and practice it together.

Linda Gonzalez is talking to a clerk at a cell phone store.

 Ask your partner the questions below. Then share your answers with another pair or the class.

Facts	What is Linda doing? What are the differences between the two plans?
Feelings	How does she feel about the two plans?
And You?	How do you make decisions about things you buy?
Comparisons	Is shopping in the United States different than in your native country? How?

Your Turn

Now write or tell the story in your own words.

Vocabulary

Look at the pictures and read the words below with a partner. Talk about what the words mean. Use a dictionary if you need it.

breakdown   **cell phone**   **local**   **long-distance**   **personal use**   **guarantee** = a promise from a company that the product will work

Your Words

in case = if
to include = to have, to come with

_____

_____

Exercise 1 The National Cellular clerk told Linda all about cell phones. Complete the sentences. Write the correct word on the line. Use the words above to help you.

1. My car had a _____ on the road, and I was late for work.

2. This phone has a two-year _____. If it breaks, we will give you a new phone.

3. We _____ free long distance with all of our phones.

4. You don't need to dial the area code for a _____ call.

5. I made a _____ call from Texas to Mexico.

6. Please tell me your cell phone number _____ we need to call you.

Listening

Before You Listen Read what Linda and her friend Maria found out about cell phones. What do you think Linda will buy, the basic phone or the Star 2000?

Exercise 2 Listen to the conversation. Help Linda decide which phone to buy. Write <u>yes</u> or <u>no</u> on the line.

_____ 1. The basic phone costs $199.

_____ 2. The Star 2000 phone comes in only bright red.

_____ 3. Linda and Maria like black phones.

_____ 4. The Star 2000 phone has a one-year guarantee.

_____ 5. Linda thinks that Roberto will like the Star 2000 phone.

After You Listen With a partner, compare your answers. Did you choose the correct cell phone?

 Your Turn

With a partner, talk about the basic and Star 2000 cell phone plans in Exercise 2. Which one is better for each person? Which phone is smaller?

SPOTLIGHT on Review Simple Present

I **use** my cell phone every day.	I **don't like** my cell phone.
You often **make** calls on your cell phone.	She **doesn't use** her old cell phone.
He always **calls** his wife on his cell phone.	
She **keeps** her cell phone in her purse.	**Does** she **use** her cellular phone every day?
We **sell** new cell phones.	Yes, she **does.**/No, she **doesn't.**
They **use** their cellular phones every day.	

Use the simple present tense to talk about events that usually happen.

I **have** a cellular phone.   She **loves** her new cell phone.   They **hate** their new cell phone.

Also use the simple present tense to talk about things that are always true.

Exercise 3 Linda wants the cell phone plan that best fits her needs. Complete the sentences. Use the correct verb in the simple present.

Linda ____doesn't have____ **(1) not have** a cellular phone. Her husband and her

sisters all _____ **(2) have** cellular phones, so she asked about prices at

National Cellular. National Cellular _____ **(3) offer** two different

plans. The Basic Plan _____ **(4) cost** $15 a month for 30 minutes. The

500 Plan _____ **(5) give** customers more minutes. Linda

_____ **(6) think** the plans are expensive.

Exercise 4 In your notebook, write a paragraph about something you don't have, but want. Use simple present. For example, write "I don't have a cell phone, but I want one. I don't want to pay a lot of money."

Pair Work

Listen to the conversation between Linda and a clerk at a different cell phone store. Then practice it with a partner.

Linda: I'd like to find out about your calling plans.

Clerk: Great. With our plan, you get 1000 minutes a month for only $29.95. That includes long distance and a money-back guarantee if you don't like the phone or the service.

Linda: That's great!

Clerk: Do you have any questions about our cell phones?

Linda: No. Thank you very much for the information.

Talk About It

In a group, talk about what you do when you want to buy something expensive. Do you look in many different stores? Where? Do you look at newspaper ads? Do you ask anyone for advice? Who? Share your group's ideas with the class.

Reading for Real

Linda Gonzalez read brochures about cell phones from National Cellular. She thought that their plans were a little too expensive, so she also got information from OptiCall Cellular.

National Cellular
After the Holidays SALE

Now you and your family can get the cell phone plan that's right for you.

Basic Plan—$15 per month
- 30 minutes of talk time free each month
- 10¢ for each additional minute
- All U.S. long distance is free
- Free voicemail

Budget Telephone: $30

500 Plan—$30 per month
- 500 minutes of talk time free each month
- Additional minutes cost only 10¢
- All U.S. long distance is free.
- Free voicemail

A2340 Telephone: Free

See your local National Cellular Store for details and to pick up your phone.

OptiCall Cellular
Folks and Family Sale

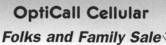

We have a very special cell phone sale for people on the go!

Special Economy Plan—$12.00 per month

You get 60 minutes per month for local calls. More minutes cost just 15¢ per minute. U.S. long distance costs 5¢ per minute. The telephone costs only $20. Voicemail is available for $2 per month.

 Exercise 5 Linda Gonzalez doesn't plan to make a lot of calls on her cell phone. She doesn't want to use long distance. Read the ads again. Complete the chart. Which plan is best for Linda? Why?

| | National Cellular | | OptiCall Cellular |
	Basic Plan	500 Plan	Economy Plan
Free minutes of talk time			
Extra minutes			
Long distance			
Voicemail			
Telephone			
Cost per month			

 ## Talk About It

In a group, ask and answer these questions.
What kind of cell phone plan do you want? Do you want a lot of minutes? Do you need voicemail? Do you need free long distance? Look at the information on the calling plans in Exercise 5. Choose the plan that is best for you. Tell your group your reasons for choosing this plan.

Scene 2: Conversation

Read the scene with a partner. Listen to the conversation and practice it together.

Linda found the right cell phone for her. Now she's using it to call her friend Maria.

 Ask your partner the questions below. Then share your answers with another pair or the class.

Facts	Where is Linda? What is she doing?
Feelings	How do you think Linda and Maria feel about the prices at Stan's?
And You	Would you like to shop at Stan's?
Comparisons	Is Stan's more or less expensive than where you usually shop?

Your Turn

Now write or tell the story in your own words.

Vocabulary

Look at the pictures and read the words below with a partner. Talk about what the words mean. Use a dictionary if you need it.

coupon   **discount**   **on sale**

double coupon day = on this day, if you bring a 25-cent coupon, you will get 50 cents off the price
metropolitan (area) = a city and the towns around it
out of (something) = not have any more
a special = something is on sale at a lower price
wonderful = really good

Exercise 6 Linda and Maria had a long talk about sales and coupons. Complete the sentences. Write the correct word on the line. Use the words above to help you.

1. Today these CD players are _____ for $159. That's a savings of $40!

2. If you buy 10 cans of tomato sauce, you get a _____ of 50 percent.

3. With this _____ you will get $1 off your total supermarket bill.

4. Savings Center is having _____ on towels. They are $3.00 off.

5. With _____, you will save even more at Stan's Discount Store!

6. I don't see any of the film that's on sale. I think that we're _____ it.

Listening

Before You Listen With a partner, look at the sentence starters and endings below. Do you think the sale prices are good?

Exercise 7 Sometimes sales are advertised on the television or radio. Listen to the information about the sale. Circle the letter of the phrase that makes each sentence true.

1. All VCRs at Family Electronics are
   a. $50.
   b. 50 percent off.
   c. the regular low price.

2. Televisions are
   a. $20 off the regular price.
   b. 20 percent off.
   c. at the low regular price.

3. Family Electronics
   a. has a special on cell phones.
   b. has cell phones from five companies.
   c. has free long distance on all cell phone calling plans.

4. Family Electronics
   a. is out of film and batteries.
   b. film and batteries are on sale.
   c. you get double coupons for film and batteries.

After You Listen With a partner compare your answers. Were your answers correct?

Your Turn

With a partner, talk about sales and discounts at your favorite stores. Which stores have the most sales? Which stores have the best discounts? How do you find out about sales?

SPOTLIGHT on Order of Adjectives

Number	Quality	Size	Age	Color	Material	Noun
four	beautiful	big	new	yellow	wood	tables
many	ugly	narrow	old	black	metal	chairs

Use this order when more than one adjective describes a noun.

Ms. Williams bought a **big new black plastic** purse.
The storm ruined our **four beautiful yellow rose** bushes.

Exercise 8 Linda went on a shopping trip. Complete the sentences. Write the adjectives in the correct order.

1. Linda bought an _____ *inexpensive, small, new* _____ cell phone.
   (new, small, inexpensive)

2. She has had _____ conversations on it.
   (interesting, many, long)

3. She received _____ bills from the cell phone company.
   (long, expensive, two)

4. She went to the cell phone store and talked to the _____ clerk.
   (helpful, young)

5. The clerk explained _____ plans to Linda.
   (new, several)

6. He showed her _____ cell phones too.
   (expensive, two, new)

Exercise 9 Linda is shopping at a second-hand store. In your notebook, write the words in the correct order to describe the items she sees there.

1. dresser   antique   wood   *antique wood dresser*
2. teapot   copper   old
3. large   trash can new   plastic
4. metal   shelves   tall   red
5. chair   leather   brown   small
6. old   black   dirty   shoes
7. cheap   red   two   purses
8. coffee maker black   plastic   nice

Your Turn

Give your partner the names of three objects. Ask your partner to describe each of them with two adjectives. Write the descriptions in your notebook. Then share them with the class. Are the words in the right order?

SPOTLIGHT on Present Participles as Adjectives

Present Participle as Adjective	Verb
I need to shop for a new **calling** plan.	to call
These are **amazing** discounts.	to amaze
He watched part of an **exciting** movie in the video store.	to excite
We don't like **boring** TV shows.	to bore

A present participle ends in **-ing.** Many present participles can be used to describe nouns.

Exercise 10 Linda and Maria decided to go shopping. Complete each sentence with a present participle used as an adjective. Use the information above to help you.

1. Linda is looking for a _____calling_____ (call) plan.

2. She found several _____ (interest) plans.

3. She thinks that having a cell phone is _____ (excite).

4. She has _____ (fascinate) conversations with all of her friends.

5. For Linda, talking on her new cell phone is never _____ (bore).

6. But when she got her bill, she made a _____ (surprise) discovery.

7. They talked for 2 hours, not 30 minutes. The cost was _____ (shock).

Exercise 11 In your notebook, write a paragraph about something you bought recently and how you feel about it. Use present participles as adjectives. For example, write "Last week I bought a brand-new purple cell phone. I love calling people on my new cell phone because it's inexpensive, and I have a lot of free minutes. It's purple, so I can find it in my backpack easily."

Pair Work

Listen to the conversation between Linda and Maria. Then practice it with a partner.

Maria: What did you buy your sister for her birthday?
Linda: A videotape of a fascinating movie. She loves it.
Maria: What movie was it?
Linda: It was *Godzilla Meets the Space Monster.*
Maria: I thought that movie was boring.
Linda: No. It's very exciting.

Talk About It

In a group, talk about something you bought recently and how you feel about it. Use your paragraph from Exercise 11 to help you. Use present participles as adjectives.

Understanding Tables

The Coupon Council is an organization that studies coupon use and that encourages companies and individuals to use coupons. **Read the information from the Coupon Council.**

1 billion = 1,000,000,000

People used 3.9 billion coupons in 2001.
The average value of a coupon is about 80¢.

Coupon Use According to Income	
Income	Percentage of People Who Use Coupons
under $25,000	72%
$25,000–$50,000	79%
$50,000–$75,000	82%
$75,000+	78%

Coupon Use According to Age	
Age	Percentage of People Who Use Coupons
18–24	70%
25–34	78%
35–44	82%
45–54	79%

People use coupons to buy many different products. This table shows the most popular kinds of coupons in 1999 and 2000.

Category	2000 rank	1999 rank
House Cleaners	1	1
Condiments and Sauces (ketchup, mayonnaise, gravy)	2	3
Frozen Foods	3	7
Medicines	4	4
Paper products	5	8

Sources: NCH NuWorld Marketing Limited and CMS/INMAR Enterprises

Exercise 12 **Maria wants to know as much about coupons as she can. Use the information from the tables to answer the questions below in your notebook.**

1. How many coupons were used in 2001?
2. What percentage of people 18–24 used coupons?
3. Which group of people use coupons more often: people who earn less than $25,000 or people who earn $50,000 to $75,000?
4. What is the average coupon worth?
5. What do most people buy with coupons?
6. What is something people don't use coupons for?

7. Did people buy more food or medicine with coupons? Why do you think so?
8. Why do you think that most people ages 35–44 use coupons?

Talk About It

In your group, talk about how many people use coupons for food, for personal items (like shampoo), and for household items (like dish soap). Write the answers you hear. Next, make a table to show the results. Follow the examples above. Use information from all the groups to create a class table.

Issues and Answers

Maria wrote to Ms. Moneybags. Read the letter and Ms. Moneybag's advice. Then talk with other students about the advice. Do you agree? What other advice can you give?

 *Ask Ms. Moneybags*

DEAR MS. MONEYBAGS,

My husband and I work really hard to make enough money for our family. He is a truck driver and I am a teacher's aide in a school. We try to save money, but at the end of the month, we hardly have any money. It's very frustrating. I would like to save money, so that I can buy a big, beautiful new car for our family. However, it seems like every month we end with no money in the bank.

Signed,

—NO MONEY

DEAR NO MONEY,

There are lots of interesting ways to save money on your daily expenses. An easy way to save money is to use coupons. You can use coupons at supermarkets, drug stores, fast-food restaurants, and many other stores. The average value of a coupon is 80 cents. It may not seem like much money, but it adds up quickly. If you use 10 coupons every week, that's $8.00. In a month, you could save more than $30! You can find many coupons in the Sunday newspaper. Remember, you always need to have your coupons with you. Keep them in your wallet, so they are always available.

Good luck,

—MS. MONEYBAGS

 Your Turn

No Money and her husband need to save money. Help No Money and her husband solve their problem.

Step 1: With a partner, list three places in your neighborhood that No Money can use coupons.

Step 2: In your notebook, write to No Money and tell her what she can buy at each place using coupons. Use your information from page 34 to help you.

Step 3: Share the places and the list of things to buy with the class.

Community Involvement

A preferred customer card is a great way to save money. These days many stores have preferred cards, not just supermarkets. Many drug stores, discount stores, and even home-improvement stores have preferred cards.

Your Turn

With a partner, make a list of places where you shop. Include discount stores, grocery stores, clothing and department stores, and any other store you shop in regularly. Next to the store name, write the kinds of things you usually buy there. If you use coupons or a preferred card at the store, put a check next to the name of the store.

Community Action

Step 1: With a partner, call two stores without checks on your list and ask if they have coupons or sales. Does either store have double coupon days? Find the answers to the following questions. Write them in your notebook.

· Can you get a preferred card?
· What do you need to do to get one?
· When is the next sale?

Step 2: Visit one store from your list that has preferred cards. Ask for a copy of the form you need to fill out to get a card. Bring it to class. What kind of information does the form ask for?

 Talk About It

In a group, talk about the information you found. Which stores have preferred cards? Which preferred cards do you want to get? What stores did you learn about? Is it better to use coupons or a preferred card? Why?

Wrap Up

Linda decided to save money by using coupons. The money she saved helped her buy an inexpensive cell phone. How do you save money on things you buy? In your notebook, make an idea map like the one below. Use ideas from this unit. Use your own ideas too.

With a partner, talk about products you want to buy. Use the simple present, present participles as adjectives, and adjectives in the correct order. Use ideas from your idea maps to help your partner save money. For example:

A: I found two amazing new watches.

B: How much are they?

A: They're eighty dollars each.

B: That's expensive! Do you think they might be on sale at Stan's Discount Store?

A: I don't know. Let's check the ad.

B: I hope they're on sale. I don't like spending too much money.

Practice your conversation. Then share it with the class.

Think About Learning

Check (✔) to show your learning in this unit. Write one more thing at the bottom.

SKILLS / STRUCTURES	PAGE	EASY 😊	SO-SO 😐	DIFFICULT 🙁
Talk about coupons, sales, and discounts	26, 30			
Understand sale ads on the TV and radio and conversations about purchases.	27, 31			
Use simple present	28			
Read and compare newspaper sale ads	29			
Use adjectives in the correct order	32			
Use present participles as adjectives	33			
Read and create a table to express information	34			
Write about places in your community to use coupons	35			
Learn about stores in your community that offer preferred cards	36			

unit 4 Trouble at Home

 ## Scene 1: Conversation

Read the scene with a partner. Listen to the conversation and practice it together.

Joan is worried because her kids argue a lot. She's asking her friend Ana for advice.

You look worried, Joan. What's the matter?

It's my kids. They argue all the time. Now that they're teenagers they constantly disagree. I hate all the fighting.

Well, it's not unusual for teenagers to argue. What do they argue about?

Everything. But mostly their chores. Every morning they argue about watching their little brother after school. Then at dinner they argue about washing the dishes.

I have an idea. Tell them to make a schedule for the week every Sunday night. Tell them to write it down and put it on the refrigerator door. That should settle the disagreement.

I can't wait to try out your suggestion!

 Ask your partner the questions below. Then share your answers with another pair or the class.

Facts	What is Joan telling Ana? What are Joan's children doing?
Feelings	How does Joan feel? Why?
And You?	What do you do when you have a disagreement at home?
Comparisons	Do children in your native country argue with their parents? about what?

Your Turn

Now write or tell the story in your own words.

Vocabulary

Look at the pictures and read the words below with a partner. Talk about what the words mean. Use a dictionary if you need it.

Your Words

_____

_____

teenagers   to agree   to disagree   to argue

constantly = happens all the time
What's the matter? = What's the problem?
chores = work people have to do
to compromise = to end a disagreement, each person gives up part of what he or she wants

to settle (something) = to end (something)
to try out (something) = to test something

Exercise 1 Joan has a few problems with her family. Complete the sentences. Write the correct word on the line. Use the words above to help you.

1. Joan's children are not babies. They are _teenagers_ .

2. Joan's children need _to agree_ about who will watch their brother after school. They both need to decide who will babysit.

3. The children need to find a way _to compromise_ . Each person needs to give up something.

4. They have some _chores_ to do: do the laundry and make the beds.

5. Joan's children _constantly_ argue about their chores. They fight all the time.

Listening

Before You Listen Read the chores in the chart below. Do you think Joan's children share their chores equally?

Exercise 2 Joan's children, Tony and Donna, are talking about their chores. Listen and complete the schedule. Write <u>Tony</u> or <u>Donna</u> in the chart.

Day	Watch Billy	Wash Dishes
Monday		
Tuesday		
Wednesday		
Thursday		
Friday		

After You Listen With a partner, compare your answers. Were you right about who did more chores?

Your Turn

A compromise is an agreement between two people. Each person gives up some of what he or she wants. With a partner, ask and answer these questions. Did Tony and Donna compromise about the schedule? Do you think that the new schedule will stop the arguments? Why?

SPOTLIGHT on Commands

Stop arguing! **Put** the schedule on the refrigerator door!
Don't leave your little brother alone.
Don't forget to check the schedule every morning.

Use commands to tell other people what to do or what not to do. Commands can be for one person or many people, but the form is the same. The subject **(you)** is not stated.

Let's make a schedule for our chores.   **Let's not fight** in front of Billy.

To include yourself in the command, use **let's**.

Exercise 3 Tony and Donna disagree about more than just chores. Write sentences telling them what to do. Use commands.

1. Donna talks on the phone for hours at a time.
   Don't talk on the phone for more than 20 minutes.

2. Tony fixes a snack for Billy after school. He doesn't clean the kitchen.
   Clean the kitchen after preparing a snack

3. Donna stays in the bathroom for an hour every morning.
   Don't stay in

4. Tony leaves his shoes in the living room.

   _____

5. Tony and Donna argue during breakfast and dinner.

   _____

6. Tony and Donna don't help Billy with his homework.

   _____

Exercise 4 In your notebook, make a list of "house rules" for your family or your roommates. Use commands and commands with <u>let's</u>. Make rules for the bathroom, the telephone, or the kitchen. For example, write "Clean the bathroom every day. Don't talk on the phone too long. Let's go to the grocery store on Tuesday."

 Pair Work

Listen to the conversation between Joan and Tony. Then practice it with a partner.

Joan: Tony, let's talk for a moment.
Tony: Sure. What's the matter?
Joan: You and Donna are always arguing about your chores.
Tony: What can I do? Donna always disagrees with me.
Joan: She says *you* disagree with *her*. Compromise and make a schedule.
Tony: OK. I'll talk to her.

 Your Turn

With a partner, role-play a conversation about house rules between two roommates. **One person is unhappy.** Use commands and the rules from Exercise 4 to help you. Share your conversation with the class.

Reading for Real

Joan's children don't argue constantly anymore, but she still wants to understand them better. She found a book about how to talk to her kids.

Settling Family Disagreements Before They Start

by Dr. Frank B. Byrd and Dr. Joyce L. Byrd

Parents face hundreds of issues that they never faced in the past. Do you have any of these problems in your family?

- Your children do not want to go to college. You think it's important for them to go.
- You are worried about your children's friends.
- Your son or daughter is having trouble in school.
- Your children argue a lot.

You can stop disagreements before they start. Improve your everyday communication with your children.

This book will teach you

- To talk to your children about any topic.
- To set regular times to talk about school, friends, and other topics.
- To talk to your children about the dangers of drugs and alcohol.
- To help your children feel proud of their ethnic heritage.

About the Authors
The husband-wife team of Dr. Frank B. Byrd and Dr. Joyce B. Byrd help families who visit their office, attend their presentations, and watch their popular TV show.

Exercise 5 Joan can't decide if she should buy this book. Read the back cover again. Circle the letter of the correct answer for each question below.

1. Who is the book for?
   a. children
   b. parents
   c. other relatives

2. What problems do the families have?
   a. problems with money
   b. problems with children
   c. problems with cars

3. How do the doctors help the families?
   a. They help them communicate better.
   b. They help them talk to the police.
   c. They help children get into college.

4. Where can you get the doctors' advice?
   a. You can listen to their radio show.
   b. You can read their book.
   c. You can write them a letter.

5. Which problem can the doctors solve?
   a. Your son is not interested in school.
   b. Your daughter keeps catching colds.
   c. Your wife thinks your son needs a car.

6. Where can you see the doctors?
   a. on TV
   b. at a bookstore
   c. in their book

Talk About It

In a group, ask and answer these questions. What kinds of problems do you think these doctors can solve? Who else can help with family problems? Should families try to solve problems by themselves? Why?

Read the scene with a partner. Listen to the conversation and practice it together.

Joan's children are not fighting anymore. But she is worried about her mother-in-law.

 Ask your partner the questions below. Share your answers with another pair or the class.

Facts — Where are Joan and Ana? What are they talking about?

Feelings — Does Joan feel better about her kids? Why? What is she upset about now?

And You? — What do you do when you have a problem with an older relative?

Comparisons — Do people from your native country have problems like this one?

Your Turn

Now write or tell the story in your own words.

Vocabulary

Look at the pictures and read the words below with a partner. Talk about what the words mean. Use a dictionary if you need it.

| senior | meal | upset | to get (lunch) | to get along | to get away (from his job) | to get out (of the hospital) |

father-in-law = the father of your husband or wife
mother-in-law = the mother of your husband or wife
relative = person in your family

Exercise 6 Joan is trying different solutions to her family problems. Complete the sentences. Write the correct word on the line. Use the words above to help you.

1. Ana and Joan never argue. They always _____.

2. Tony and Donna have to take care of Billy after he _____ of school every day.

3. Joan is _____. She is worried about her mother-in-law.

4. Joan's husband's mother is her _____.

5. Joan wants _____ from work and take a day off.

6. Joan's parents are _____ citizens. They are 70 years old.

Listening

Before You Listen Read about Joan's mother-in-law and Meals on Wheels. Why is Joan asking for help?

Exercise 7 Joan is calling Meals on Wheels for her mother-in-law. Listen to the conversation. Circle the letter of the phrase that makes each sentence true.

1. Joan's mother-in-law is
   a. 78 years old.
   b. 87 years old.
   c. 88 years old.

2. Joan's mother-in-law
   a. cannot walk.
   b. cannot stand up for long periods.
   c. cannot eat.

3. Meals on Wheels
   a. only delivers lunch.
   b. delivers breakfast and lunch.
   c. delivers lunch and dinner.

4. Meals on Wheels
   a. is free.
   b. costs $4 a day.
   c. costs between $1 and $4 a day.

After You Listen With a partner, compare your answers. Did you predict why Joan is asking for help?

Talk About It

In a group, ask and answer these questions. Should Joan sign her mother-in-law up for Meals on Wheels? Why? Do you know any people who could use the help of Meals on Wheels? Do you know other groups like Meals on Wheels?

SPOTLIGHT on Review *May* and *Might*

I **may call** Meals on Wheels.

You **might want** some help with your family.

Joan **may ask** Meals on Wheels to help her mother-in-law.

Meals on Wheels **might start** delivery tomorrow.

Joan's mother-in-law **may not go** home for a few weeks.

Joan's mother-in-law **might not like** the food from Meals on Wheels.

Use **may** and **might** to talk about actions that are possible or probable.

Donna **may use** this computer to do her homework.

Tony **may not use** the computer to watch a movie.

Use **may** for permission.

Exercise 8 After calling Meals on Wheels, Joan talks to Ana about her mother-in-law. Rewrite the sentences using <u>may</u> or <u>might</u>.

1. I think that she will go home in a few weeks.
   <u>She may go home in a few weeks.</u>

2. I think she will sign up for Meals on Wheels.
   _____

3. I think that Meals on Wheels is the answer to her problem.
   _____

4. I think that the delivery person is ringing the doorbell right now.
   _____

5. I don't think that she will pay a lot for Meals on Wheels.
   _____

6. I think that my mother-in-law will like Meals on Wheels.
   _____

7. I don't think that she will need Meals on Wheels when she feels better.
   _____

8. I think she will be able to cook for herself.
   _____

Exercise 9 People are always thinking about what may or may not happen in the future. In your notebook, write what you think may happen tomorrow. What might you do? Use <u>may</u>, <u>may not</u>, <u>might</u>, and <u>might not</u>.

 Your Turn

With a partner, talk about ways people could solve problems at home. Use **may** and **might.** For example, say "My son is having trouble in school. I may call his teacher tomorrow to find out how to help him with his homework."

I'd **better** start dinner. The kids will be home soon.
You **should** call Meals on Wheels. You **shouldn't** go home at lunch every day.
She **ought to** get some help with her mother-in-law.
We **ought to** talk to a family counselor.
They **had better** call Meals on Wheels right away. **They'd better not** forget.

Use **should** to give advice. Use **ought to** for strong advice.
Use **had better** for very strong advice.

Exercise 10 Joan needs some advice. Read the statements below. Write a sentence to help her solve the problems. Use <u>should, shouldn't, ought to, had better</u>, and <u>had better not</u>.

1. My mother-in-law can't cook for herself.
   You'd better call Meals on Wheels.

2. I am tired from helping my mother-in-law all the time.
   _____

3. My teenage children always argue about chores.
   _____

4. My teenage children argue about the telephone too.
   _____

5. Tony doesn't study very much after school.
   _____

6. Sometimes Tony doesn't wash all of the dishes.
   _____

Exercise 11 Ana's kids don't do their homework, and they don't listen carefully to the teacher. Her son is only interested in playing football, and her daughter is only interested in talking to her friends on the telephone. In your notebook, write some advice for Ana. Use <u>should, shouldn't, ought to, had better</u>, and <u>had better not</u>.

 Pair Work

Listen to the conversation between Ana and Joan. Then practice it with a partner.

Ana: My children are having trouble in school. What should I do?
Joan: You ought to call their teacher.
Ana: I'd better call her soon. They are not getting good grades.
Joan: You should call today before you forget.
Ana: They shouldn't be having trouble in school. They are good students.
Joan: The teacher should be able to explain the problem.

 Talk About It

In a group, talk about the kinds of problems families have. What do parents argue about? What do children argue about with parents? What should families do when they have problems?

Understanding Pie Charts

Many older adults live alone. Often they do not have much money. Many of them cannot go shopping or cook. Meals on Wheels helps these older adults by bringing them hot meals every day. Here are some facts about Meals on Wheels.

> About 27 percent of older adults are poor.
> There are about 20,000 Meals on Wheels programs in the United States.
> Nationwide, Meals on Wheels delivered about 100,000,000 meals in 2001.
> On average, people who get Meals on Wheels are women 75 years of age or older.

Here is some information about where older adults live.

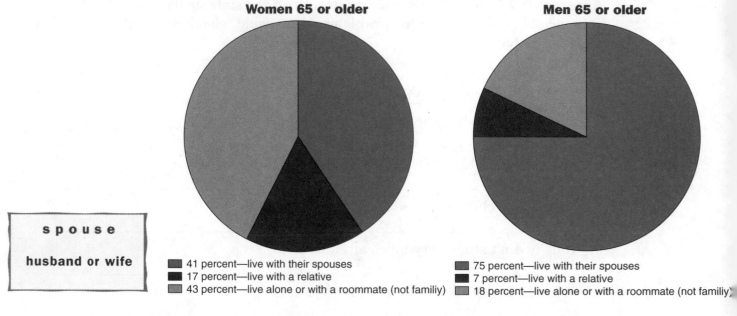

Women 65 or older   **Men 65 or older**

spouse

husband or wife

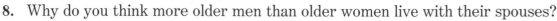

■ 41 percent—live with their spouses
■ 17 percent—live with a relative
■ 43 percent—live alone or with a roommate (not familiy)

■ 75 percent—live with their spouses
■ 7 percent—live with a relative
■ 18 percent—live alone or with a roommate (not familiy)

Exercise 12 Joan decided to pay Meals on Wheels to deliver lunch to her mother-in-law. In your notebook, answer the following questions.

1. What problems do older adults have?
2. What percentage of older adults are poor?
3. About how many meals did Meals on Wheels deliver in 2001?
4. Which person probably lives alone, a man or a woman?
5. Which person is probably a Meals on Wheels customer, an older man or an older woman?
6. What percentage of older women live alone?
7. What percentage of older men live alone?
8. Why do you think more older men than older women live with their spouses?

Talk About It

In a group, talk about where the older adults in your families live. Do they live with their spouses? with a relative? alone? with a roommate? Make two pie charts, one for male relatives and one for female relatives. Include your grandparents and your parents, if they are more than 65 years old. Are your results the same as the pie chart above? Share your pie charts with the class. Use the information to create a class pie chart.

Issues and Answers

Joan's husband wrote to Abdul and Anita. Read the letter and Anita's advice. Then talk with other students about the advice. Do you agree? What other advice can you give?

Ask Abdul and Anita

DEAR ANITA,

I am very worried about my neighbor, Miss Werner. She is very old and she is alone a lot. My wife and I help her, and so do others. However, she feels sad and lonely because she is home all day and has very few friends. What can we do to help Miss Werner?

—CONCERNED NEIGHBOR

DEAR CONCERNED NEIGHBOR,

Many older adults like to go to senior centers during the day. Older adults can go there to play games, sew, exercise, or talk. Last year, the senior center in our town organized trips to museums, famous restaurants, and to a large shopping mall.

Older adults who need extra help can use Meals on Wheels or senior daycare. Meals on Wheels brings hot meals to older adults every day. Senior daycare is a place for older adults who need extra help during the day. The adults stay at the center all day while their relatives are at work. Adults who need care all of the time can move to a nursing home where nurses are always there to help them.

Talk to your neighbor about services in your community like Meals on Wheels, the senior center, and senior daycare. I am sure that you can find a solution to your friend's problem!

Good luck,

—ANITA

 Your Turn

Concerned Neighbor wants to help Miss Werner. What advice should he give her about services for older adults in his community?

Step 1: With a partner, talk about the four kinds of help mentioned in the letter: senior centers, senior daycare, Meals on Wheels, and nursing homes. Which one may be best for Miss Werner? Why?

Step 2: In your notebook, write a few sentences explaining the reasons for your choice. For example, write "Concerned ought to tell his neighbor about senior centers. She is lonely, and she can have friends there. He shouldn't tell her about nursing homes. She isn't sick."

Step 3: Share your sentences with the class.

Community Involvement

There are many special services for families. Meals on Wheels helps people who cannot shop and cook for themselves. Senior centers provide older adults with a fun place where they can enjoy themselves.

Your Turn

With a partner, think of problems that families in your community might have. Think of money problems, health problems, school problems, and other kinds of problems. Make a list.

Community Action

Step 1: Share your list of family problems with another pair. Make one group list. Decide which problems are the most important, and write those at the top.

Step 2: With your group, choose one of the top problems you wrote on your group list. Find a special service in your community that helps people with that problem. Use the telephone book, the newspaper, or the Internet. Find the following information about the service, and write the answers in your notebook:
- Name of the service
- Address
- Phone number
- Hours
- What services do they provide?
- Are there any fees?
- Are there any services in your native language?

Talk About It

In a group, talk about the services you found for the important problem on your list. Which special services can help you with the other problems on your list? Did you find services that may help someone you know?

Wrap Up

Joan used a book to solve the problem with her children, and Meals on Wheels to help her mother-in-law. Work with a partner. In your notebook, make a T-chart like the one below. Fill in the T-chart with problems that families like yours might have. Then write advice for the problems.

Problem	Advice
Daughter's new friends	talk to your daughter

With a partner, talk about problems with a family member. Use ideas from your T-chart, commands, **may, might, should, ought to,** and **had better.** Use words from this unit. For example:

A: I'm feeling a little worried these days.

B: What's the matter?

A: Well, my daughter stays out too late at night. She doesn't do her chores, and I don't like her new friends.

B: You can't let her be with the wrong friends. She might get into trouble.

A: She says she is old enough to choose her own friends and I should not bother her.

B: You ought to talk with her right away. Explain that she may get in trouble. She may be upset, but she'd better find some new friends.

Practice your conversation. Then share it with the class.

Think About Learning

Check (✔) to show your learning in this unit. Then write one more thing you learned.

SKILLS / STRUCTURES	PAGE	EASY ☺	SO-SO 😐	DIFFICULT ☹
Talk about problems at home	38, 42			
Understand conversations about family problems	39, 43			
Use commands and commands with **let's**	40			
Read a book jacket for information	41			
Use **may** and **might** to talk about the future	44			
Use **should, ought to, had better** to give advice	45			
Read and create a pie chart to express information	46			
Understand information about family community service options	47			
Learn about local community resources for everyone in your family	48			

Scene 1: Conversation

Read the scene with a partner. Listen to the conversation and practice it together.

Thuy just got a promotion at her job. She's finding out about the benefits.

Ask your partner the questions below. Then share your answers with another pair or the class.

Facts	What are Thuy and her boss talking about?
Feelings	How does Thuy feel? Why?
And You?	What benefit do you need the most?
Comparisons	In your native country what benefits do people receive from their jobs?

Your Turn

Now write or tell the story in your own words.

Vocabulary

Look at the pictures and read the words below with a partner. Talk about what the words mean. Look up the words in a dictionary and write the meanings in your notebook.

dental insurance

disability insurance

health insurance

premium

flextime

paid sick days

personal day
co-payment
life insurance
promotion
too
either

Your Words

_____

_____

Exercise 1 Thuy's coworkers have the same benefits she does. Complete the sentences. Write the correct words on the line. Use the words above to help you.

1. I need a _____ to go downtown and pay some parking tickets.
2. Francisco was a receptionist. Now he's a file clerk. He got a _____.
3. Marlene needs to see a dentist. Her _____ will pay for the visit.
4. Mark has _____. If he dies, his son will still be able to pay for college.
5. Juan needed his _____. He didn't work for a month after he broke his leg.

Listening

Before You Listen Read about the benefits below. What benefits do you think Thuy's boss will talk about?

Exercise 2 Listen to Thuy's boss telling her about her new benefits. Complete the sentences with the missing information.

1. After _____ year(s) of employment, you get 10 paid vacation days.

2. The insurance plan has a high _____, but you can go to any doctor.

3. Some insurance plans cost a lot, but have low _____ for office visits.

4. With _____ you can work longer for four days a week. Then you get three days off.

5. If you are a good assistant manager, you might get a _____ to manager.

After You Listen With a partner, **compare your answers.** Did you hear the correct information?

Your Turn

With a partner, talk about flextime. Could you have flextime at your job? Write the perfect schedule for you. Share your schedule with the class.

SPOTLIGHT on Review Comparative and Superlative Adjectives

The fee for Health Insurance Plus is **higher than** the fee for regular health insurance.
The family plan has the **highest** fee of all the plans.
Use **-er** and **-est** to compare most adjectives of one or two syllables.

Health Insurance Plus is **more** expensive **than** regular health insurance.
The family plan is the **most** expensive.
We use **more** and **most** to compare most adjectives of more than two syllables.

Full-time employees have **better** benefits **than** part-time employees.
Sunshine Coffee and Tea Company has the **best** benefits.
Remember, some adjectives are irregular.

Exercise 3 Read about Thuy's new job. Write the correct form of the adjective on the line. Use **-er**, **-est**, **more**, or **most**. Write <u>the</u> or <u>than</u> as needed.

Last week Thuy got a promotion to full-time assistant manager. The benefits are

_____ *better* _____ **(1) good** she had before. Her pay is _____

(2) high before too. However, her hours are _____ **(3) long** before.

Her new job is _____ **(4) difficult** her old job too. However, Thuy says

Sunshine Coffee and Tea is _____ **(5) good** company in town.

Exercise 4 Look at the benefits chart. In your notebook, write the sentences with the correct form of the comparative or superlative. Write <u>the</u> or <u>than</u> as needed.

Benefit	Employee Only	Employee and Husband or Wife	Family Plan
Health Insurance	$45	$75	$100
Dental Insurance	$12	$22	$33
Life Insurance	Free	Free	Free

Health insurance is **(1) expensive** dental insurance. The family plan is the **(2) expensive** option. If you have a large family, the family plan is **(3) good** option for you. This year my insurance premiums are **(4) big** last year's, because my wife and I had a baby. Life insurance is the **(5) cheap** benefit—it's free!

 ## Pair Work

Listen to the conversation between Thuy and her brother Sang. Then practice it with a partner.

Thuy: Now I'm a full-time employee, so I get health insurance. We didn't have health insurance before.

Sang: That's great. We don't have insurance either. I need a job with benefits.

Thuy: Well, maybe you should apply at my company. We're hiring right now.

Sang: I'd love to work there. Your benefits are much better than mine.

 ## Your Turn

With a partner, create a list of all the benefits you can think of. Which benefits are most important to you and your partner? Number your ideas in order of importance starting with 1 as the most important. Share your list with the class.

Reading for Real

Thuy began full-time work at Sunshine Coffee and Tea. Read the memo that she got from the Human Resources Director.

> **To:** Thuy Nguyen
> **From:** Human Resources Director, Sunshine Coffee and Tea
> **Date:** May 6
> **Re:** Benefits
>
> Congratulations on your full-time job at Sunshine Coffee and Tea. Full-time employees get the following benefits:
>
> - 7 paid holidays a year
> - 5 paid vacation days a year
> - 1 paid personal day a year
> - 5 paid sick days a year
>
> Also, you will get health insurance, dental insurance, and life insurance. Our medical and dental insurance have low premiums and co-payments.
>
> For many of these benefits, you must fill out forms. Please stop in the Personnel Office to fill out the benefit forms before the end of the month.

Exercise 5 Full-time employees at Sunshine Coffee and Tea use their benefits every day. Read the memo again. Write the name of the benefit on the line.

_____ 1. Nick wanted Thanksgiving Day off with pay.

_____ 2. Francis stayed home with a cold for two days, but he got paid.

_____ 3. Nancy broke her arm. She got paid while she stayed home for 10 days to get better.

_____ 4. Stan's daughter needed braces on her teeth. He only had to pay a co-payment.

_____ 5. Pat needed a day off for some medical tests.

_____ 6. Francesca wanted a day off because it is a holiday in her native country. The holiday is not celebrated in the United States.

 Talk About It

In a group, talk about the benefits listed above. Which benefits in the memo are important for you? Why? Was Thuy's change from part-time to full-time work a good idea? Why or why not?

Scene 2: Conversation

Read the scene with a partner. Listen to the conversation and practice it together.

Thuy and Alicia are going in to work.

 Ask your partner the questions below. Then share your answers with another pair or the class.

Facts — Where are they going? Why is Thuy holding the door open for Alicia?

Feelings — How does Alicia feel about the new baby? How does she feel about her job?

And You? — Have you ever taken a leave from a job? Explain.

Comparisons — In your native country, when parents have a new baby, do they take family leave from work?

Your Turn

Now write or tell the story in your own words.

Vocabulary

Read the words below with a partner. Talk about what the words mean. Look up the words in a dictionary and write the meanings in your notebook.

401 (k)	daycare	disability leave
company-sponsored	in advance	family leave
contribution	to provide	personal leave
		tuition reimbursement

Exercise 6 Alicia read about the company's benefits. Complete the benefits chart. Write the name of the benefit in the space.

Benefit	Description and Cost	
	The company will provide a free place where employees may keep their children while they are at work.	
	If you cannot work for several weeks because of a personal problem, you will be able to come back to your job. Your time off must be approved by your supervisor in advance.	
	Employees may attend company-sponsored school.	
	With this savings plan, you can save money to help pay the cost of your retirement. The company also makes contributions.	
	If you cannot work for several weeks because of a physical problem, you can stay home and still receive 75 percent of your regular pay. Cost: Premium is one percent of your paycheck.	
	After you have a new baby, you can take up to six weeks of leave without pay. This benefit is for both mothers and fathers. Cost: Free	

 # Listening

Before You Listen Look at the pictures and read the answers below. What kinds of benefits do you think the employees will talk about?

Exercise 7 Sunshine Coffee and Tea employees are talking about their lives. Listen to the information. Circle the letter of the benefit each person needs.

1.
   a. family leave
   b. company-sponsored daycare
   c. personal leave

2.
   a. tuition reimbursement
   b. personal day
   c. daycare

3.
   a. paid holidays
   b. paid sick days
   c. 401 (k) contribution

4.
   a. disability insurance
   b. life insurance
   c. dental insurance

After You Listen With a partner, compare your answers. Did you choose the correct benefits?

 ## Talk About It

In a group, ask and answer these questions. Do you have benefits at work? Which ones? Which benefit do you use the most? Why? Which benefits do you want to have at work? Why?

SPOTLIGHT on Comparative and Superlative Adverbs

Use the comparative and superlative forms of adverbs to compare actions.

Bill arrives at work **earlier** then Alan.
Bill and Mary work **more carefully** than Per and Alan.
Bill and Mary work **faster** than Per and Alan too.

Most adverbs that end in **-ly** form the comparative with **more** + the adverb. Some one syllable adverbs form the comparative by adding **-er** to the adverb.

She works **the most carefully.**
She works **the fastest,** too.

Most adverbs that end in **-ly** form the superlative with **most** + the adverb. Some one syllable adverbs form the superlative by adding **-est** to the adverb.

Exercise 8 As an assistant manager, Thuy has to watch her employees work. Complete the sentences. Use comparative and superlative adverbs. Use <u>the</u> as needed.

1. Julia works ___more carefully___ (careful) than Alicia.

2. This machine runs _____ (fast) of all the machines in the shop.

3. John talks _____ (loud) than Ms. Grimes.

4. Frank works _____ (hard) of everyone in the company.

5. Please try to work _____ (quiet). You're disturbing the customers.

6. Of all the employees, Miguel always speaks to the customers _____ (polite).

7. We're working very fast and making lots of mistakes. Please try to work _____ (slow).

8. Ko is always late for work. She needs to get up _____ (early).

Exercise 9 In your notebook, write the names of three classmates. Then write sentences that compare the students. Use comparative and superlative adverbs. For example, write "Carlos writes faster than Leslie. Oscar writes the fastest."

 In Your Experience

In your notebook, write five sentences about things you do well. Compare yourself to your relatives, friends, and classmates. Share your sentences with the class. For example, write "I work the hardest of everyone at my company."

SPOTLIGHT on Review Too + Adjective

He's **too sick** to go to work. He needs to stay home.
She's **too busy** to fill out the insurance forms. She has to do it later.

Remember, **too + adjective** means more than you need or want.

Exercise 10 Thuy's new job makes her too tired to stay up late at night. Look at the pictures. Write a sentence. Use <u>too</u> + adjective.

1. (busy) _He's too busy to eat._

2. (tired) _____

3. (messy) _____

4. (noisy) _____

5. (hot) _____

6. (late) _____

Exercise 11 You got a promotion and just received a lot of information about benefits. How do you feel about your benefits? In your notebook, write five sentences with <u>too</u> + adjective. For example, write "I am too confused to choose a 401 (k) plan."

 Pair Work

Listen to the conversation between Thuy and the Human Resources Director. Then practice it with a partner.

Thuy: Thank you for all the information about benefit plans. But right now I'm too confused to choose.

Director: Really? Maybe I can help you. What are you confused about?

Thuy: Well, with the 401 (k) plan, do I have to contribute 15 percent of my pay?

Director: No, you can contribute any amount up to 15 percent of your pay.

Thuy: Maybe I should only contribute 5 percent. 15 percent is too much. I need money for bills right now.

 Your Turn

With a partner, role-play a conversation between an employee and a Human Resources Director about benefits. Use **too** + adjective and words from this unit. Share your conversation with the class.

Understanding Line Graphs

One of the best ways to save for retirement is a 401 (k) plan. With this kind of plan, you make regular contributions to a savings account. Your employer makes contributions too. The money you put in is not taxed.

You can save a lot of money if you contribute regularly to a 401 (k) plan. Imagine that you contribute $2,000 each year to one of these plans. The line graph tells you how much you will have after 1, 10, 20, and 30 years (at four percent interest).

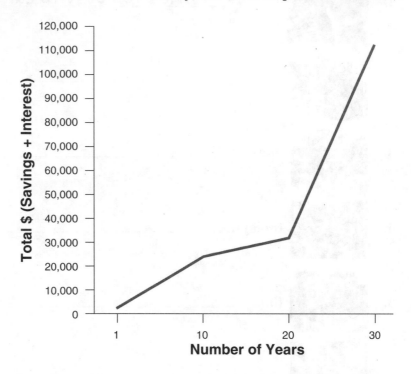

Exercise 12 Thuy decided to read more about 401 (k) plans. In your notebook, answer the following questions.

1. What do 401 (k) plans help people do?
2. Why do people need to save money for retirement?
3. Do you have to pay tax on money you put in a 401 (k) plan?
4. If your contribution is $2,000, how much will you have (with interest) after one year?
5. If your contribution is $2,000 each year for 10 years, how much will you have (with interest)?
6. How much more will you have if you contribute the same amount for 20 years (with interest)?
7. If your contribution is $2,000 each year for 30 years, how much will you have (with interest)?
8. You should start giving money to your 401 (k) as soon as possible. Why?

 ## Talk About It

In a group, talk about retirement plans. How many employers offer 401 (k) programs? How many people use them? Make a line graph showing how much money your group would have if each person contributed $10 each month for two years at four percent interest.

Issues and Answers

Thuy wrote to Ms. Moneybags. Read the letter and Ms. Moneybags' advice. Then talk with other students about the advice. Do you agree? What other advice can you give?

 Ask Ms. Moneybags

DEAR MS. MONEYBAGS,

I just started a new full-time job at my company. My employer gave me a lot of forms to fill out, but I don't understand all of them. One is for a 401 (k) account. What is that? I didn't sign up because I don't know what it is. Today I heard a coworker talk about borrowing money from her 401 (k) to pay for her child's college education. I think I might want a 401 (k) now. Did I make a mistake?

—WONDERING

DEAR WONDERING,

You shouldn't sign things you don't understand, but a 401 (k) is a good thing. This is a way for you to save for your retirement or your kids' college education. Money is taken from your paycheck before taxes. Some companies may put extra money in your account. Put as much money as you can in your 401 (k). The best part is that you do not pay tax on the money you put into your account.

The laws may be different depending on your immigration status. Find out from your bank or employer if your immigration status changes the way the account works.

Best Wishes,

—MS. MONEYBAGS

 Your Turn

Wondering is thinking about signing up for the 401 (k) at her new job. Explain to Wondering why she should do that.

Step 1: With your partner, look at the information and graph on page 58. Why is it important to save for retirement? How can a 401 (k) help you save?

Step 2: Write a few sentences about why a 401 (k) plan is the best way to save for retirement. For example, write "Wondering should sign up for a 401 (k) because her employer will put in extra money."

Step 3: Share your sentences with the class.

Community Involvement

One of the things that makes a job good is the benefits. With benefits such as health insurance, dental insurance, disability insurance, family leave, and so on, your life will be easier. However, not all jobs have good benefits. How can you find jobs with good benefits?

Price Club Employee Benefits

Your Turn

With a partner, think of ways benefits can help you. Then write the five most important benefits you have or want to have.

Community Action

Step 1: Share your list with another pair. Make one group list. Decide which benefits are the most important, and write those at the top.

Step 2: With your group, make a list of the companies you or your family members work for. Talk about what benefits each company offers for full-time and part-time employees. If you don't know about your company benefits, ask an employee of the company, or use the telephone book, the newspaper, or the Internet. Write the information in the chart below.

Name of Company	Benefits for Full-time Employees	Benefits for Part-time Employees

Talk About It

In a group, talk about the information you found on each company. Which companies provide the best benefits? Which companies provide the benefits that you need? Do you want to apply to any of these companies? Which ones? Share your ideas with the class.

Wrap Up

After talking with friends and coworkers, Thuy decided to sign up for the 401 (k) plan. Retirement plans are only one benefit offered by employers. With a partner, make a chart like the one below about benefits in your notebook. Fill it in.

Benefits I Get	Benefits My Partner Gets
Benefits We Both Get	Benefits Neither of Us Gets

Imagine that you are a human resources director at Sunshine Coffee and Tea. Use the information above to write a memo explaining the benefits your company provides. Use **too + adjective,** comparative and superlative adjectives and adverbs. Use words from this unit. For example:

Memo

To: New Employees

From: Human Resources Director, Sunshine Coffee and Tea

RE: Benefits

Welcome to Sunshine Coffee and Tea, the fastest growing company in the United States. Here is a list of the benefits we offer full-time employees:

Share your memo with the class.

Think About Learning

Check (✔) to show your learning in this unit. Write one more thing at the bottom.

SKILLS / STRUCTURES	PAGE	EASY ☺	SO-SO 😐	DIFFICULT ☹
Talk about different kinds of benefits	50, 54			
Understand information about insurance and benefits	51, 55			
Use comparative and superlative adjectives	52			
Read a company memo about benefits	53			
Use comparative and superlative adverbs	56			
Use **too** + adjective	57			
Read and create a line graph to express information	58			
Write about the benefits of a 401(k)	59			
Learn about the benefits offered by employers in your community	60			

Scene 1: Conversation

Read the scene with a partner. Listen to the conversation and practice it together.

Todd and Feng are organizing a heritage festival at their children's school.

 Ask your partner the questions below. Share your answers with another pair or with the class.

Facts	What are Todd and Feng doing?
Feelings	How do they feel about the Heritage Festival? How do you know?
And You?	If you were in a heritage festival, what could you show from your native country?
Comparisons	Does your town have festivals for different cultures? Which ones?

Your Turn

62   Now write or tell the story in your own words.

Vocabulary

Look at the pictures and read the words below with a partner. Talk about what the words mean. Look up the words in a dictionary and write the meanings in your notebook.

festival   immigrant   potluck dinner   talent show   to perform

almost	heritage
already	team
just	to become
yet	to observe (a holiday)

Your Words

_____

_____

to set up

Exercise 1 Todd and Feng like to organize events for their town. Complete each sentence. Write the correct word on the line. Use the words above to help you.

1. We are going to organize an international music _festival_.

2. Several bands and singers are going to _perform_.

3. We've _already_ sold a lot of tickets. Yesterday we sold 25 tickets.

4. We had a _team_ of five people working together to organize the Heritage Festival.

5. Carlos will read a poem from Mexico so people can learn about his _heritage_.

6. The dinner will begin in five minutes. The food is _almost_ ready.

 ## Listening

Before You Listen With a partner, read the statements about people getting ready for the Heritage Festival. Do you think they are ready?

Exercise 2 Listen to the volunteers at the festival. Have they finished all the work yet? Write yes or no on the line.

_____ 1. They've already turned on the lights in the auditorium for the talent show.
_____ 2. They haven't put the food for the potluck dinner on the table yet.
_____ 3. They've already put a big sign in front of the school.
_____ 4. They haven't put up the all the decorations yet.
_____ 5. They've already set up a room for small children to play in.

After You Listen With a partner, compare your answers. Were Feng and Todd ready for the festival?

 Your Turn

With a partner, decide which of the actions in Exercise 2 need to be done before the festival opens, and which can be done after. Share your answers with the class.

SPOTLIGHT on Present Perfect with *Already, Yet,* and *Just*

I **have (I've) unlocked** the door.
You **have (You've) organized** the festival.
He **has (He's) put** a sign in front of the school.
She **has (She's) put** a sign in front of the school.
It **has (It's) started.**

We **have (We've) unlocked** the door.

They **have (They've) organized** the festival.

Form the present perfect with the present of **have** and a past participle. Most past participles are the same as simple past. See page 122 for a list of common past participles.

Use the present perfect with **already** and **yet** to tell if recent actions happened before now or will happen in the very near future.
She's already arrived at the Heritage Festival.
She **hasn't put** the food in the kitchen **yet.**
Use the present perfect with **just** to emphasize that the action happened very recently.
I've just performed at the Heritage Festival.

Exercise 3 Look at the to-do list for the festival and answer the questions. Check marks mean the activity is completed. Use present perfect with <u>already</u> or <u>yet</u>.

cook food
eat lunch
✔ have talent show
✔ set up tables & chairs
take down tables & chairs
✔ have games for kids

1. Have people seen the talent show yet?
   Yes, they've already seen the talent show.

2. Have people eaten lunch yet?

   _____

3. Have they set up the tables and chairs yet?

   _____

4. Have they taken down the tables and chairs yet?

   _____

5. Have the kids played games yet?

   _____

Exercise 4 What customs and traditions have you just observed? In your notebook, write five sentences with <u>just</u>. For example, write "We've just celebrated Mexico's Independence Day. It's September 16th."

Pair Work

Listen to the conversation between Todd and Feng. Then practice it with a partner.

Feng: We haven't celebrated Chinese New Year yet. But I'm already hungry!

Todd: Do you have special foods for New Year's?

Feng: Yes. My favorite is a vegetable dish called <u>jai</u>.

Todd: I haven't tried that yet. I'm going to try it this year.

Feng: It's really good. You'll like it.

In Your Experience

In your notebook, write about customs and traditions in the United States that you have or haven't observed. Use the present perfect with **already, yet,** and **just.** For example, write "I haven't eaten turkey on Thanksgiving yet. I've already seen the Fourth of July fireworks."

fireworks

Reading for Real

As part of the Heritage Festival, Todd and Feng's children read about immigrants in the United States.

join
be part of

Image courtesy of Harp Week LLC

The United States has always been a country of many cultures. Before Europeans came to North America, many groups of Native Americans lived here. Different Native American groups had different cultures. The first Europeans in the United States were from England and Holland, but immigrants came from all European countries. Many people also immigrated from Asia and Africa. Sadly, many Africans were brought to the United States as slaves. Many immigrants come from Latin America too. Today, the United States has people from more cultures than ever.

In the 19th century, people spoke of the United States as a "melting pot." People thought that all immigrants should forget their native cultures and languages and become English-speaking Americans. They felt that people should assimilate—join American culture. However, not everyone wanted to assimilate completely. Many people tried to keep parts of their cultures, such as foods, customs, and languages. However, their children often forgot their parents' or grandparents' language. But most Americans, even those whose families have been here a long time, can tell the countries their relatives came from. And of course, new immigrants take great pride in their culture and language.

For all of these reasons, melting pot is no longer a good way to describe the United States. Instead, people now call the United States a "salad bowl." They say salad bowl because in a salad, you can still see all of the individual parts (lettuce, tomato, and so on), but all the different parts are mixed together and begin to take on the flavor of one another.

Exercise 5 What did the children learn about immigrants? Read the textbook again. Write yes or no on the line.

Yes 1. The United States has always been a country of many cultures.

_No_ 2. All immigrants to the United States have assimilated completely.

_No_ 3. The "melting pot" is an accurate way to describe the United States.

Yes 4. When families assimilate completely, the children and grandchildren forget their first language and culture.

_No_ 5. Immigrants to the United States do not take pride in their cultures and traditions.

_No_ 6. People call the United States a "salad bowl" because Americans do not like immigrants.

 Talk About It

In a group, ask and answer these questions.
Do you think newcomers to the United States should assimilate completely (melting pot) or only partially (salad bowl)? How can you help your family have pride in your native culture and language?

Scene 2: Conversation

Read the scene with a partner. Listen to the conversation and practice it together.

The Heritage Festival was a big success. Two months later, Todd is talking to Feng outside his house.

 Ask your partner the questions below. Then share your answers with another pair or the class.

Facts	What are Todd and Feng talking about?
Feelings	How does Feng feel about the Chinese New Year?
	How does Todd feel?
And You?	What do you like to do to celebrate the New Year?
Comparisons	How do people celebrate the New Year in your native country?
	When is it?

Your Turn

Now write or tell the story in your own words.

Vocabulary

Read the words below with a partner. Talk about what the words mean. Look up the words in a dictionary and write the meanings in your notebook.

culture	to bring luck	to gather
custom	to celebrate	to prepare
tradition	to expect	to send off
traditional		

Exercise 6 Todd and Feng learned about many different customs and cultures. Complete the sentences. Write the correct word on the line. Use the words above to help you.

1. Some people think that seeing a rainbow will _____.

2. The _____ food to serve on Thanksgiving Day is turkey.

3. Americans _____ New Year's Day on January 1st.

4. I _____ to celebrate the Chinese New Year in China this year.

5. A lot of people _____ at the school last week for the festival.

Listening

Before You Listen With a partner, look at the pictures and read the sentence starters below. Which cultures do you think people are talking about?

Exercise 7 Listen to the conversations about family, heritage, and tradition. Circle the letter of the phrase that best completes the sentence.

1.  In Frank's family, it's a tradition to
   a. eat lunch together on Sunday.
   b. go to church.
   c. bring food to your grandmother's house.

2.  Aziza does not want to paint the front door white because
   a. painting doors brings bad luck.
   b. blue doors bring good luck.
   c. blue is her favorite color.

3. Komiko wants her daughter to study flower arrangement because
   a. it is important in Japanese culture.
   b. she can use these skills to get a job.
   c. her daughter needs help in school.

4.  Mr. Lang wants Mrs. Sok to perform because
   a. she has performed for large audiences before.
   b. storytelling is important in her culture.
   c. she is famous.

After You Listen With a partner, compare your answers. Were you right about the cultures people talked about?

Your Turn

With a partner, talk about your favorite traditions or customs from your native country. Make a list and share it with the class.

SPOTLIGHT on the Present Perfect with *Ever* and *Never*

I've **celebrated** the Chinese New Year a number of times.
He **has gone** to Hong Kong.
They **have attended** many different festivals.

Use the present perfect to talk about whether people have done things at any time in the past. Use it to emphasize that the past experience is important today.

Have you **ever** been to Hong Kong?	Yes, I have been to Hong Kong.
Has she **ever** seen the fireworks?	No, she has **never** seen the fireworks.
Have they **ever** eaten Korean food?	No, they have **never** eaten Korean food.

Use the present perfect with **ever** in questions to ask if someone has done something even one time in his or her whole life. If he or she has done it even once, he or she must answer yes. If he or she has not done it even one time, use **never**.

Exercise 8 Feng and his friends are talking about which customs and traditions they have experienced. Write the correct form of the verb on the line. Use <u>never</u> if needed.

1. I ___have celebrated___ (celebrate) Thanksgiving three times.
2. _____ you ever _____ (be) in an international festival?
3. Mrs. Garfield _____ (never try) Russian food.
4. _____ they ever _____ (perform) their dances for you?
5. She _____ (never be) to New York.
6. I _____ (attend) the city heritage festival many times.
7. He _has never eaten_ (eat) at the festival.
8. _Have_ you ever _seen_ (see) the parade before?

Exercise 9 Ask the students in your class the questions below. For each question, find one person who answered yes, and write his or her name in your notebook.

1. Have you ever performed with a choir?
2. Have you ever lived in New York?
3. Have you ever repaired a car?
4. Have you ever gotten lost on your way to school?
5. Have you ever been on television?
6. Have you ever gone to a potluck dinner?
7. Have you ever been to a Thanksgiving celebration in the United States?
8. Have you ever tried food from another culture?
9. Have you ever used a computer to send e-mail to your native country?
10. Have you ever ridden a horse?

Your Turn

With a partner, talk about your experiences living in the United States. Use the information in Exercise 9 to help you. For each question with a yes answer, ask your partner "What happened?" Share your partner's answers with the class.

SPOTLIGHT on Present Perfect with *For* and *Since* and Simple Past

He **lived** in China from 1999 to 2003.
(He doesn't live there now.)

Past   Now   Future

Use the simple past for actions that started and ended at a specific time in the past.

She **has lived** in China for 5 years. (She moved there 5 years ago. She still lives there today.)
They **have lived** in China since 1999. (They started to live there in 1999. They still live there today.)

Past   Now   Future

Use the present perfect to talk about actions that began in the past and are still happening today.
For is used to talk about how long the action has taken.
Since is used to emphasize the time that the action started.

Exercise 10 Feng has lived in the United States since 1988. Complete the sentences. Write the correct word on the line. Use <u>for</u> or <u>since</u>.

Feng has lived in the United States **(1)** _____for_____ many years. He has worked for TelTronics Industries **(2)** _____for_____ six years.

(3) _____Since_____ last year, he has been a manager. Feng has been married

(4) _____since_____ 2000. His wife is from Hong Kong, but she has lived in

California **(5)** _____since_____ she was 10 years old.

Exercise 11 What are some interesting things you have done since you came to the United States? In your notebook, write five sentences in the present perfect with <u>for</u> or <u>since</u>. For example, write "I have celebrated Thanksgiving since 2001. I have gone to the fireworks every year for three years."

Pair Work

Listen to the conversation between Feng's wife and their neighbor, Dao-Ming. Then practice it with a partner.

Po-Yan: How long have you lived here, Dao?
Dao-Ming: I've lived in California for three years. Before that I lived in Georgia.
Po-Yan: When did you come to the United States?
Dao-Ming: I've lived in the United States since 1992. How long have you been here?
Po-Yan: Oh, a long time. I was born in Hong Kong but I've lived in California since I was 10 years old.

Talk About It

In a group, ask and answer these questions. Use the present perfect with **for** or **since**. How long have you lived in the United States? How long have you had your current job? How long have you studied English? How long have you lived in this city? How long have you been in this class?

Understanding Pie Charts

Todd was born in the United States, but Feng was born in China. He is an immigrant. The United States has always been a nation of immigrants. Right now, 28.4 million people in the United States were born in another country. That's about 10.4% of the U.S. population. Where do all of these immigrants come from?

Native Countries of U.S. Immigrants, 2000

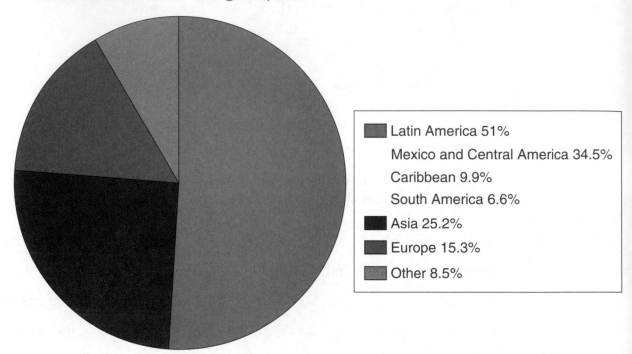

- Latin America 51%
  - Mexico and Central America 34.5%
  - Caribbean 9.9%
  - South America 6.6%
- Asia 25.2%
- Europe 15.3%
- Other 8.5%

Exercise 12 Feng read a newspaper article about the different cultures in his city. In your notebook, answer the following questions.

1. What region of the world do most U.S. immigrants come from? Name a country from that region.
2. What country do most U.S. immigrants come from?
3. What percentage of U.S. immigrants are from Europe?
4. What percentage of U.S. immigrants are from Asia?
5. Do many immigrants come to the United States from Australia? Why do you think so?
6. Which place are more immigrants from, the Caribbean or South America?
7. Based on the pie chart, do you think the United States has many immigrants from China?
8. About 8.5% of immigrants are from places not named on the pie chart. Name a country that some of these immigrants might be from.

Talk About It

In a group, find out where your classmates came from. Write the answers you hear. Next, make a pie chart to show the results. Follow the example above. Use information from all the pie charts to create a class pie chart.

Issues and Answers

Todd's friend Emilio wrote to Abdul and Anita. Read the letter and Abdul's advice. Then talk with other students about the advice. Do you agree? What other advice can you give?

Ask Abdul and Anita

DEAR ABDUL,

I am very worried about my children. We moved here from Mexico 12 years ago. Our children were very young when we moved here. They don't remember anything from Mexico. All of their friends are American. My kids hardly speak Spanish. Last week, they refused to go to a party to celebrate May 16, which is an important holiday for all Mexicans. And now they don't want to visit their grandmother in Mexico this summer. They want to go to computer camp. I feel like I am a bad parent because my kids don't love Mexico. What should I do?

—UPSET

DEAR UPSET,

Of course you want your kids to be proud of their heritage. Here are some ways to help them learn about their heritage:

1. Find some local organizations and activities related to your native country. You might go to a church in Spanish, see a film in Spanish, or attend the meeting of a club.

2. Since your kids love computers, ask them to show you how to look up information on Mexico on the Internet in Spanish and in English.

3. Compromise about the trip to Mexico. Maybe they can study computers in Mexico. Or they can go to computer camp for half the summer and visit their grandmother the other half.

Sincerely,
—ABDUL

Your Turn

Upset needs to share information with his children about their heritage.

Step 1: With a partner from your native country, make a list of things your children should know about their heritage. Include information such as your native country's region of the world, the number of U.S. immigrants from your country, important people in the history of your native country, and important people in the United States from your native country.

Step 2: Use the Internet, newspapers, or books in English or your native language to find the information you identified in Step 1.

Step 3: Share the information you found with the class. Why do you think it's important for children to know these things?

Community Involvement

Many American towns have events and resources to find about different cultures. Festivals like this one share food, music, and other customs from countries around the world.

Your Turn

With a partner, think about your neighborhood in the United States. How many different cultures do you see there each week? Make a list of the different cultures in your community.

Community Action

Step 1: With a partner, choose one interesting culture from your list. Do not choose your own culture. Use the Internet, the newspaper, or the phone book to find events and resources for that culture. An event can be a festival, concert, or a meeting of a club or organization. A resource can be a business, a newspaper, or an organization.

Step 2: Write a description of one event and one resource in your notebook. Answer the following questions.
  · To which culture do the event and resource belong?
  · What is the name of the event?
  · What does it celebrate?
  · When and where does it happen?
  · What is the name of the resource?
  · Who does it help?
  · What does it do for people from that culture?

Talk About It

In a group, read your page, and explain the events and resources you found. Do you want to try any of the events and resources for your culture? For other cultures? Which ones? Share your ideas with the class. Use your information to create a class book about all the cultures in your community.

Wrap Up

Feng wants his children to be proud of their Chinese heritage. With a partner, make an idea map like the one below in your notebook. Write about ways that you and your families can feel proud of your cultural heritage and traditions.

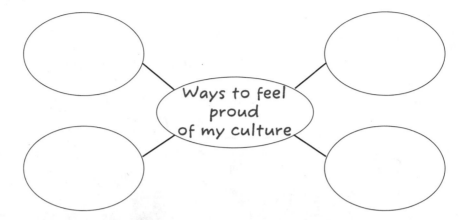

With a partner, talk about your experiences with different cultures. Use present perfect with **ever, never, for, since, already, yet,** and **just.** Use words from this unit. For example:

A: So how long have you lived in the United States?

B: I've lived here since January 2002.

A: Really? Have you ever been to San Francisco?

B: No, I've never been there, but I've been to Los Angeles three times already.

A: I never miss the festivals in San Francisco's Chinatown.

B: I just heard about those. I'm making plans to go there for New Year's.

Practice your conversation. Then share it with the class.

Think About Learning

Check (✔) to show your learning in this unit. Then write one more thing you learned.

SKILLS / STRUCTURES	PAGE	EASY 😊	SO-SO 😐	DIFFICULT 😞
Talk about customs and traditions from your native country	62, 66			
Understand conversations about preparations and different cultures	63, 67			
Use the present perfect with **already yet,** and **just**	64			
Read about immigration in the United States	65			
Use the present perfect with **ever** and **never**	68			
Use the present perfect with **for** and **since**	69			
Read and create a pie chart to express ideas	70			
Write about ways to help children have pride in their heritage	71			
Learn about cultural events and resources in your community	72			

Scene 1: Conversation

Read the scene with a partner. Listen to the conversation and practice it together.

Al Ramos is visiting Dr. Izumi for his yearly medical checkup.

 Ask your partner the questions below. Share your answers with another pair or the class.

Facts	Is Al's diet healthy? What does the doctor tell him?
Feelings	How does Al feel about his weight?
And You?	Is your diet healthy? How do you know?
Comparisons	Do people eat junk food in your country? What kinds?

Your Turn

Now write or tell the story in your own words.

Vocabulary

Look at the pictures and read the words below with a partner. Talk about what the words mean. Look up the words in a dictionary and write the meanings in your notebook.

Your Words

_____

_____

blood pressure   junk food   stress   to gain weight

checkup   heart attack   to go on a diet   at risk
cholesterol   operation   to recommend

Exercise 1 Al started to read the brochures his doctor gave him. Complete the sentences. Write the correct word on the line. Use the words above to help you.

1. Too much _____ can make you fat.

2. He's going to _____ in order to lose 25 pounds.

3. You should see your doctor for a _____ every year.

4. Too much _____ can make you feel nervous and angry.

5. Overweight people are _____ for a heart attack.

Listening

Before You Listen Look at the pictures and read the advice below. What should the people do to improve their health?

Exercise 2 Listen to Dr. Izumi and her patients. Circle the letter of the best advice for each patient.

1.
  a. Get more sleep.
  b. Eat less junk food.
  c. Get more exercise.

2.
  a. Change her diet.
  b. Take medicine.
  c. Get more exercise.

3.
  a. Get a different job.
  b. Don't drink so much coffee.
  c. Get more exercise.

4.
  a. Stop working so much.
  b. Have an operation.
  c. Get more sleep.

After You Listen With a partner, compare your answers. Did you know what the people should do to improve their health?

Your Turn

With a partner, talk about the health problems an unhealthy lifestyle can cause. Complete the chart in your notebook.

Problem	Causes
heart attack	high cholesterol, stress

SPOTLIGHT on Present Perfect Progressive

```
|——————————————————|——————————————|
Past                  NOW
```

I've (I haven't) been eating a lot of junk food lately.
You've (You haven't) been watching TV a lot too.
She's (She hasn't) been buying a lot of candy.
It's (It hasn't) been getting more difficult to eat healthy.

We've (We haven't) been gaining weight lately.

They've (They haven't) been thinking about changing their diets.

Have **you been eating** carefully?

Yes, I have./No, I haven't.

Use the present perfect progressive to talk about actions that began in the past and continue up to the present. The actions may or may not continue into the future.

Exercise 3 Al and his wife have been arguing about Al's diet. Complete the sentences. Write the correct word on the line. Use the present perfect progressive.

1. Al _____has been gaining_____ (gain) weight lately.

2. His wife thinks that he _____ (eat) too much.

3. He _____ (buy) a lot of junk food.

4. On the other hand, his wife _____ (lose) weight.

5. She _____ (eat) a lot of fruit and vegetables.

6. She _____ (try) to get Al to go on a diet.

7. Al _____ (not listen) to her.

8. In fact, his wife thinks that he _____ (eat) more.

Exercise 4 In your notebook, write sentences about how your diet has been lately. What have you been eating and drinking? For example, write "I have been drinking too much soda. I should drink more water. I haven't been eating enough vegetables."

Pair Work

Listen to the conversation between Dr. Izumi and another patient, Kathy. Then practice it with a partner.

Dr. Izumi: Have you been eating correctly?

Kathy: Yes, I have. I've been eating a lot of fruit and vegetables.

Dr. Izumi: That's good. Have you been eating much junk food?

Kathy: Not really. I like to eat ice cream for dessert once in a while.

Dr. Izumi: That's not a problem as long as you don't do it often.

Kathy: I'll try to not eat ice cream too often. Thanks, doctor.

In Your Experience

In your notebook, write a paragraph about what you have been doing to improve your health. Use present perfect progressive. Use information from Exercise 4 to help you. Share your paragraph with the class.

Reading for Real

Al is reading more of the information that Dr. Izumi gave him. He is learning about stress, and how it is bad for his health.

Stress

Stress is one of the most common complaints doctors hear today. People may feel stress because they are too busy at work. They may also feel stress because they are worried about their children. People can also feel stress because of a change in their lives. A new job or a move to a new city can be very stressful. When people have too much stress, they say that they feel "stressed out."

Luckily, there are some simple ways to lower your level of stress.

✓Get more exercise. Try simple exercises, like going for a walk every day. Swimming, playing soccer, or running are also great ways to lower stress.

✓Watch your diet. A diet with plenty of fruit and vegetables and that is low in sugar, salt, and fat will reduce your stress.

✓Avoid too much coffee, cola, and tea. These drinks contain caffeine, which can make you feel nervous. Try to drink only two or three of these drinks each day.

✓Get enough sleep. Most people need about eight hours of sleep every night.

✓Try to relax. Listen to music, read a good book, or do something fun. You will feel much better.

✓Talk to someone. If you feel stressed at work, talk calmly to your boss or a coworker about the problem. If you feel that your children are having trouble in school, visit the teacher and talk about the problem.

 Exercise 5 **Many of Dr. Izumi's patients are trying to lower their stress. Are they doing the right thing? Read the pamphlet again. Write <u>yes</u> or <u>no</u> on the line.**

_____ 1. Chuck was under a lot of stress at his office, so he yelled at his coworkers.

_____ 2. Juanita is always worried about her kids' grades at school. She decided to call the principal to talk to him about them.

_____ 3. John was nervous about work, so he stayed up late every night to watch TV. He starts work at 5:00 in the morning.

_____ 4. Ellen was afraid that she would lose her job, so she talked to her boss.

_____ 5. Miguel wanted to relax after work, so he went to the movies with his friends.

_____ 6. Anya has two jobs; she is always tired and nervous. She drinks 10 cups of coffee every day.

 ## Talk About It

In a group, talk about what you do to reduce stress. Do you try to avoid it? Why? Do you think the advice above will help people have less stress? What other ways do people have of reducing stress? Share your answers with the class.

Scene 2: Conversation

Read the scene with a partner. Listen to the conversation and practice it together.

Carla has worked at the Belltone Company for a month, so now she can apply for health insurance. She just attended a benefits meeting.

 Ask your partner the questions below. Share your answers with another pair or the class.

Facts	How long has Carla worked at the company? What are Carla and Al talking about?
Feelings	How does Carla feel? Why?
And You?	Do you have health insurance?
Comparisons	Do most people have health insurance in your native country? Why or why not?

Your Turn

Now write or tell your story in your own words.

Vocabulary

Look at the picture and read the words below with a partner. Talk about what the words mean. Look up the words in a dictionary and write the meanings in your notebook.

certain   traditional insurance

HMO   lately

paperwork   likely

prescription
medicine

Exercise 6 Carla asked her employer for more information about HMOs. Complete the sentences. Write the correct word on the line.

1. I want to choose a _____ doctor, so I need traditional insurance.

2. Most insurance plans pay for pills and other _____.

4. I've been eating a lot of junk food _____. I need to start eating a healthy diet.

5. A heart attack becomes more _____ if you have high cholesterol.

6. I want the _____ because it is less expensive than traditional insurance.

7. When you start an insurance plan, you have to fill out a lot of _____.

8. Both types of insurance usually pay for _____ from the pharmacy.

Listening

Before You Listen Read the statements about health insurance. What do you think Carla learned at the meeting?

Exercise 7 Listen to the Human Resources Manager and find out the differences between an HMO and traditional insurance. Write <u>HMO</u> or <u>T</u> on the line.

_____ 1. You can go to any doctor you want.

_____ 2. You don't pay for regular check-ups.

_____ 3. You have to go to certain doctors.

_____ 4. It costs less.

_____ 5. You can go to any hospital you want.

_____ 6. Prescription medicine is free.

After You Listen With a partner compare your answers. Does Carla have enough information now to make a decision about health insurance?

Talk About It

In a group, ask and answer these questions. Which do you prefer, traditional insurance or an HMO? Why? Use the information from Exercise 7 to help you. Do you like a certain doctor? Do you need to save money? Share your ideas with the class.

SPOTLIGHT on Review Past Progressive

Carla was reading.

She asked   She asked   She asked   NOW

While Carla **was reading** the insurance information, **she asked** a number of questions.
Carla **was attending** the benefits meeting **when** Al **was cleaning** the supply room.

Use the past progressive to talk about actions that happened over time in the past. Use clauses with **when** and **while** to talk about other actions that interrupt something that happened over time in the past, or occur at the same time.

She was filling out the insurance form.

She made a mistake.   NOW

While she was filling out the insurance form, she **made** a mistake.

If the clause with **when** or **while** comes first, we use a comma after it.
If the clause with **when** or **while** comes second, do not use a comma.

Exercise 8 It is important to get information before deciding what health plan to use. Complete the sentences. Write the correct form of the verb on the line. Use the simple past or past progressive.

1. While Al _____was getting_____ (get) a checkup, he _____found_____ (find) out he needed to go on a diet.

2. While Carla _____ (attend) the benefits meeting, she _____ (learn) about the insurance plans.

3. When Al _____ (clean) the supply room, Carla _____ (attend) the meeting.

4. While the speaker _____ (talk), Carla _____ (complete) some of the paperwork.

5. Carla _____ (not make) any mistakes while she _____ (fill) out the paperwork.

6. While Carla _____ (turn) in the forms, she _____ (met) the head of human resources at the company.

Exercise 9 In your notebook, write five sentences about what you did the last time you took a day off, and what was happening at work while you were gone. Use simple past and past progressive with when and while. For example, write "While I was reading the newspaper at breakfast, my coworkers punched in and started to work."

 Talk About It

In a group, talk about what happened on your day off. Use the sentences you wrote in Exercise 9 to help you. For example, say "When my coworkers were driving home, I was in a restaurant."

SPOTLIGHT on the Past Progressive and the Present Perfect Progressive

She was living in Chicago when she got married.

She got married.

|_____•_____|

She was living in Chicago.   NOW

Use the past progressive for actions that occurred over time in the past, but have now ended. The specific starting and ending time is not important.

She's been living in the same house for 42 years.
I've been cleaning the supply room for an hour.

|_____|

I've been cleaning the   NOW
supply room for an hour.

Use the present perfect progressive to talk about actions that began in the past, occurred over time, and are still occurring in the present.

Exercise 10 Carla has been trying to change her diet. Complete the sentences. Write the correct form of the verb on the line. Use the present perfect progressive or past progressive.

1. Carla _____*has been dieting*_____ (**diet**) for a month now.

2. She _____ (**eat**) a lot of fruit and vegetables.

3. She _____ (**not eat**) any junk food.

4. Yesterday, everyone said that she _____ (**lose**) weight.

5. Carla said that she _____ (**feel**) better lately too.

6. She _____ (**do**) more work last week too, because she had more energy.

7. Carla _____ (**work**) very hard recently.

8. She _____ (**plan**) a vacation for a long time.

Exercise 11 In your notebook, write five sentences using the present perfect progressive and five sentences using the past progressive. For example, write "I have been going to school for six months. I was working full-time when I started school."

 Talk About It

In a group, talk about the different health care plans where you work. Are you or someone you know part of an HMO? Name one good thing and one bad thing about HMOs or the health plan where you work.

Understanding Bar Graphs

Insurance helps us pay for health care. When we have insurance, we know that our health care bills will be covered. And health care is too expensive to pay for without insurance. A doctor's visit can cost $60 or more. A simple operation can easily cost $10,000 or much more. Most people with insurance get it from their jobs, but not all jobs offer insurance. Also, people who are out of work often have no insurance.

Here is some information on health insurance coverage in the United States.

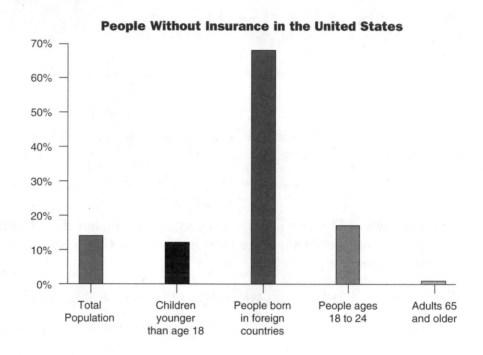

People Without Insurance in the United States

Exercise 12 Carla has been trying to learn more about health insurance. In your notebook, answer the following questions.

1. Why is health insurance so important?
2. About what percentage of people have health insurance?
3. Why do people born outside the United States often not have health insurance?
4. What percentage of children do not have health insurance?
5. What percent of senior citizens have health insurance?
6. Based on the graph, will a 70-year-old person probably have health insurance?
7. Which group of people represented on the graph has the greatest difficulty with insurance?
8. Will a teenager who moved here from Africa probably have health insurance?

Talk About It

In a group, talk about your families. How many people in your family live in the United States? How many of them have insurance? Find the number of people and then figure out the percent of people. Make a bar graph to show the results. Follow the example above. Use the information from all the graphs to create a class graph.

Issues and Answers

Carla's brother wrote to Ms. Moneybags. Read the letter and Ms. Moneybags' advice. Then talk with other students about the advice. Do you agree? What other advice can you give?

 *Ask Ms. Moneybags*

> **COBRA**
>
> temporary insurance for when people lose a job

DEAR MS. MONEYBAGS,

I have a part-time job with no benefits, and my wife had a full time job with great insurance. We get a check-up every six months, have our blood pressure and cholesterol checked, and have prescription benefits. We don't eat too much and we try not to gain weight. She just found out that her company is closing next month, so we will lose our insurance. Do we really need it?

How can we keep our insurance?

—NOT LUCKY

DEAR NOT LUCKY,

Like most Americans, you get your insurance from your job. And like most Americans, you are losing your insurance because of a change to your employment. You definitely need insurance.

You are lucky because you can plan ahead. First, sign up for COBRA. COBRA is a program that lets you pay your old employer to continue your health insurance. It requires paperwork, but you can have COBRA while your wife is looking for a new job. Second, try to save a little money in case your wife does not find a new job right away. Third, begin looking for companies in your town that offer benefits. If the company doesn't offer benefits, she should not apply there! Talk to all of your friends and neighbors. Ask them for companies that they know of that offer benefits. Check the newspaper and the employment office too.

Keep looking and you'll find something.

Sincerely,

—MS. MONEYBAGS

 ## Your Turn

Worried needs information about COBRA insurance while his wife looks for another job.

Step 1: With your partner, go to http://www.cobrainsurance.com on the Internet. Click on Questions and Answers (FAQs) and What is COBRA? Read the information.

Step 2: Write a few sentences telling Worried about the information on the web site. Tell him who can receive COBRA, how long it lasts, and what it does.

Step 3: Share the information you found with the class.

Community Involvement

Paying for health care is a problem for many people. At least 38 million people in the United States do not have health insurance. However, there are places people without insurance can go to get help in an emergency.

Your Turn

With a partner, talk about medical emergencies your family has had, or might have in the future, such as a heart attack or a broken arm. Make a list. How would these emergencies be treated in your native country? Did you have insurance?

Community Action

Step 1: Find the name of a free clinic in your area. Ask an English-speaker, or use the telephone book or the Internet. Can you get help for the emergencies you listed above?

Step 2: With a partner, call the clinic you identified in Step 1, or look at their web site. Find the answers to the following questions. Write the answers in your notebook.
- What are their hours?
- Do they have ambulance service for emergencies?
- Will they accept people with COBRA?
- Which HMO insurance do they accept?
- Can low-income families get any services free? Which ones?

Talk About It

In a group, talk about the information you found. Which health care providers can help with the health concerns in your list? Where else can you go for help with the other problems in your list? Which health care provider is best for low-income families? Ask your group for ideas.

Wrap Up

Al and Carla want to be healthy. How can people stay healthy? In your notebook, create an idea map like the one below. Write the ways you know to stay healthy.

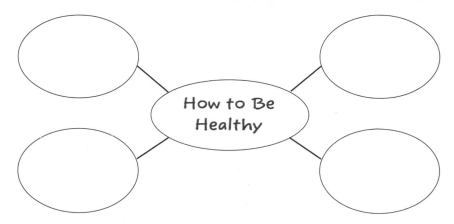

With a partner, talk about things you have or haven't been doing to be healthy. Use the present perfect, the present perfect progressive, and the past progressive. Use words from this unit. For example:

A: I've been feeling a little stressed out these days.

B: Why?

A: I need to go on a diet. I eat a lot of junk food and have been gaining weight.

B: I've thought about going on a diet, too. I was exercising a lot in the summer, but now I don't exercise at all.

A: I know it's hard to get regular exercise, but it's important.

B: We can go to the gym together. I'll call you this weekend.

Practice your conversation. Then share it with the class.

Think About Learning

Check (✔) to show your learning in this unit. Write one more thing at the bottom.

SKILLS / STRUCTURES	PAGE	EASY 😊	SO-SO 😐	DIFFICULT 😞
Talk about health insurance and ways to be healthy	74, 78			
Talk about health benefits and improving your health	75, 79			
Use the present perfect progressive	76			
Read about reducing stress	77			
Use the past progressive	80			
Understand past progressive vs. present perfect progressive	81			
Read and create a bar graph to express information	82			
Find out about COBRA insurance	83			
Learn about health care in your neighborhood	84			

Scene 1: Conversation

Read the scene with a partner. Listen to the conversation and practice it together.

Madge just bought a new hair dryer. It's not working.

Earl, look at my nice new hair dryer. I just bought it at the discount store.

I thought you didn't want to shop at that store anymore. You said there were too many problems with the merchandise.

Well, it was only $14.95. I'm going to try it.

AAAAH!

Quick! Turn it off!

You're right. Now I have to take this hair dryer back. I have to bring the receipt with me. Is it in the bag?

You see? You shouldn't shop at that store. There's always something wrong with the merchandise.

 Ask your partner the questions below. Share your answers with another pair or the class.

Facts	What are Madge and Earl talking about? What happened?
Feelings	How does Madge feel about the hair dryer? Why? How does Earl feel?
And You?	Have you ever had a problem with a purchase? What did you do?
Comparisons	What happens in your native country when people have this kind of problem?

Your Turn

Now write or tell the story in your own words.

Vocabulary

Look at the pictures and read the words below with a partner. Talk about what the words mean. Look up the words in a dictionary and write the meanings in your notebook.

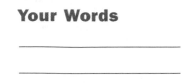

Your Words

_____

_____

label	receipt	to exchange	to return something

purchase   refund   to complain

merchandise   reputation   to expire

Exercise 1 Madge brought the hair dryer back to the discount store. Complete the sentences. Write the correct word on the line. Use the words above to help you.

1. We don't give refunds. You can _____ the dryer for something else.

2. You need a _____ to exchange these socks.

3. I bought this radio yesterday and it's already broken. I'm going to _____ about it.

4. If you have a problem with a _____, take it back to the store.

5. I'd like to get my money back for this cell phone. Please give me a _____.

6. This hamburger meat smells bad. It _____ yesterday.

Listening

Before You Listen With a partner, look at the pictures and read the phrases. How would you solve the problems?

Exercise 2 Listen to Madge's friends talk about the things they bought. Circle the letter of the phrase that best describes the solution to each problem.

1.
    a. Bring it back with the receipt.
    b. Get a refund right away.
    c. Talk to the manager.

2.
    a. Call technical support.
    b. Return it to the store for a refund.
    c. Try restarting it.

3.
    a. Check the label.
    b. Throw it away.
    c. Call the supermarket.

4.
    a. Take it to a mechanic.
    b. Repair it himself.
    c. Take it back to the dealer.

After You Listen With a partner, compare your answers. Did you correctly solve the problems?

Your Turn

With a partner, ask and answer these questions. Have you ever had a problem with a purchase? Where did you buy it? What was the matter with it? How did you feel when it happened?

SPOTLIGHT on Review *Have to* and *Should*

You **should** always keep all your receipts.
You **should** check all products carefully before you buy them.

Use **should** to make recommendations.

You **have to have** a receipt in order to get a refund.
We **have to return** this coat tomorrow. It's too small.

Use **have to** for things that are required.

They **shouldn't** shop at that terrible store.

Exercise 3 The City Department of Consumer Protection wrote this advice for consumers. Complete the sentences. Write the correct word on the line. Use <u>should</u>, <u>shouldn't</u>, or <u>have to</u>.

1. Customers _____ should _____ keep their receipts.

2. Customers _____ throw away the box until they're sure they want to keep the product.

3. Customers _____ show the receipt to get a refund or an exchange.

4. Stores _____ replace a product if the product doesn't work.

5. Customers _____ read the label before they buy a product.

Exercise 4 What should the people do? In your notebook, write sentences using <u>have to</u>, and <u>should</u>.

1. Madge's new hair dryer won't work.
2. The things that Madge buys at the discount store never work.
3. Frank is at the store to return a printer, but he doesn't have the receipt with him.
4. Wanda bought a new dress. After she took it home, she decided it was too short.
5. Mike bought a CD, but it won't play in his CD player. His other CDs work fine.
6. Francie bought some meat at the supermarket. When she got home, the meat was bad.

 Pair Work

Listen to the conversation between Earl and a friend from work. Then practice it with a partner.

José: I bought an alarm clock that doesn't work.
Earl: You should take that alarm clock back to the store. Do you have the receipt?
José: I'm not sure.
Earl: Well, you have to have a receipt to get a refund or an exchange.
José: Right. I have to check the bag. I think the receipt is still there.

 In Your Experience

In your notebook, write five sentences about something you want to return. What should you do? What shouldn't you do? Use **have to, should,** and **shouldn't** in your sentences. Share your sentences with the class.

Reading for Real

The discount store wouldn't exchange the hair dryer for Madge. The store said that she broke it. Madge knows that she did not break the hair dryer. Madge read this pamphlet about the Better Business Bureau. Now she wants to complain about the store.

The Better Business Bureau is a community organization that helps people solve problems with businesses. Almost every city and town in the United States has a Better Business Bureau.

When a customer has a major problem with a company, the customer can complain to the Better Business Bureau. The Better Business Bureau will then contact the company and try to find a solution that is good for everyone.

You can also contact the Better Business Bureau when you want to make a major purchase. You can check to see if the company has a good reputation or if a lot of customers have complained about that company in the past.

When Should You Call the Better Business Bureau?
You should call the Better Business Bureau for major problems with purchases from a store or a business. If you bought something from an individual, the Better Business Bureau cannot help you.

Filing a Complaint
First you should contact the company to see if you can resolve the problem yourself. If you cannot resolve it, then you can complain. First you fill out a form. If the Better Business Bureau thinks your complaint is justified, it will work with you and the company to help you find a solution.

 Exercise 5 Madge could call the Better Business Bureau. Should the people below contact the Better Business Bureau? Write <u>yes</u> or <u>no</u> on the line.

_____ 1. Tim wants to return a jacket, but the store won't take it back because he does not have the receipt.

_____ 2. Jesse and Luisa want to put a new roof on their home. They want to know if the roofing company has a good reputation.

_____ 3. Francie bought a used washing machine from her neighbor. After a month, the washing machine stopped working.

_____ 4. Tyrone bought four new tires for his car. The next morning the tires were flat. Tyrone doesn't have time to call the store to complain.

_____ 5. Vikki wants to buy a used car. She wants to make sure the used car dealer is honest.

_____ 6. Christine sold some old plates to an antique store. The owner promised to pay her $200 the next day, but the next day he refused to pay her.

 Talk About It

In a group, talk about a problem you have had with a purchase. Have you ever had a problem that the Better Business Bureau could help you with? What was the problem? Share your ideas with the class.

Scene 2: Conversation

Read the scene with a partner. Listen to the conversation and practice it together.

Madge and Earl bought a new car a few months ago. It's been in the shop five times, and it won't run correctly. Now Earl and Madge are at the car dealer talking about the problem.

 Ask your partner the questions below. Share your answers with another pair or the class.

Facts	What are Madge and Earl talking to the car dealer about?
Feelings	How do Madge and Earl feel about the car? Why?
And You?	Imagine that you bought a lemon. What will you do?
Comparisons	What do people in your country do when they have problems with something new?

Your Turn

Now write or tell the story in your own words.

Vocabulary

Look at the words below with a partner. Talk about what the words mean. Look up the words in a dictionary and write the meanings in your notebook.

car dealer

consumers

in the shop

lemon

lemon law

policy

protection

store credit

to get (our) money back

to run (machines)

Exercise 6 Sometimes people have to return something they bought. Complete the sentences. Write the correct word on the line. Use the words above to help you.

1. Earl's new car breaks down a lot. I think it's a _____.

2. I'm sorry, but I can't drive you to work. My car is _____.

3. That car really _____ well. It never has to be repaired.

4. You cannot get a refund. We only give _____.

5. If I cannot get another size, I want to _____ my money.

6. It is against the store _____ to give a cash refund.

Listening

Before You Listen With a partner, look at the return policy. What do you think happens if someone wants to return something?

Exercise 7 Some stores don't offer a refund when a purchase is returned. Listen to the conversation and complete the return policy.

> ## Uptown Discount Stores
>
> 1. All exchanges must be accompanied by a _____.
>
> 2. There are no _____. We only give exchanges or a store credit.
>
> 3. Consumers have _____ days from the date of purchase to request a receipt.
>
> 4. You _____ wear or use merchandise that you want to return.
>
> 5. You may not get a store credit for a video or CD if either has been opened. You can only _____ it for another copy of the same video or CD. This is because some customers copy the CD or video and then return the merchandise.

After You Listen With a partner compare your answers. Did you write the correct policy?

Your Turn

With a partner, role-play a conversation about a CD that you bought three days ago. You opened the CD, and the CD works fine. However, you don't like the music on it. Can you exchange it for a CD by a different singer? Why?

You **must** fill out a lemon law form.
You **have to** attach a copy of the receipt.

Use **must** and **have to** to talk about things that are required and necessary.

You **must not** lose the receipt.

Use **must not** to talk about things that are forbidden.

She **doesn't have to** go to the copy shop. We'll copy the receipt for her here.

Use **don't have to** to talk about things that are not necessary.

Exercise 8 Madge and Earl have problems with their new car. Complete the sentences. Write the correct word on the line. Use <u>must</u>, <u>must not</u>, <u>have to/has to</u>, or <u>don't/doesn't have to</u>.

1. Madge and Earl want to get another car. They _____ have the receipt.

2. If they want another car, they _____ fill out a form.

3. It's not necessary to make a copy of the receipt. He _____ copy the receipt.

4. The car dealer couldn't repair their car. The dealer _____ give them a new car.

5. Madge and Earl should be polite. They _____ yell at the clerk.

6. The car dealer _____ give them their money back. He can give them a different car or their money.

Exercise 9 Imagine that you work at a store. The store needs a new return policy. In your notebook, write rules for the policy. Use <u>must</u>, <u>must not</u>, <u>have to/has to</u>, or <u>don't/doesn't have to</u>. For example, write "You must have a receipt. You must not use the product before you return it." Share your rules with the class.

 Your Turn

With a partner, role-play a conversation between a clerk and a customer. Your partner is buying something from the store. You're the clerk. Explain the return policy to him or her. Use the policy you created in Exercise 9.

For example:

John: Can I return these basketball shoes?
Adnan: Yes, but you have to have the receipt. Also, you must not wear the shoes before you return them.

SPOTLIGHT on Must for Probability

The red car looks great but has been in shop 15 times. That car **must be** a lemon.

Use **must be** to talk about conditions that are probable or possible.

His new car is a lemon. He **must feel** angry.
He filled out the lemon law form. He **must want** his money back.

Use **must** with other verbs to show that we think something is probable.

Exercise 10 Sometimes people have to return things to stores. How do the people feel? Write a sentence. Use <u>must</u>.

1. Madge and Earl's car has never worked correctly.
   <u>They must be very angry.</u>

2. The salesperson is afraid that Madge and Earl will return the car.
   _____

3. The salesperson says that they can get another car.
   _____

4. The owner of the car dealership doesn't want to give Madge and Earl a different car.
   _____

5. Madge and Earl exchanged the car. Now they have a car that runs great.
   _____

Exercise 11 Earl listened to problems his friends had had. In your notebook, complete the sentences. Use <u>must</u> + verb to write what you think is true about each person.

1. John just bought a new guitar. It sounds terrible. John <u>must feel upset</u>.
2. Wadi's new car is a lemon. Wadi . . .
3. Maria's new camera doesn't work. Maria . . .
4. Customers at this store have a lot of consumer problems. The customers. . .
5. Tanya just bought a beautiful new video camera. Tanya . . .

 Pair Work

Listen to the conversation between Madge and a neighbor. Then practice it with a partner.

Madge: We just bought a new car, but I think it's a lemon.
Juanita: You must be upset. What are you going to do?
Madge: I don't know. Maybe I'll call the salesperson.
Juanita: There must be something he can do to help.
Madge: It's still new. We'll probably be able to exchange it for another car.

 Talk About It

In a group, talk about a time you returned something to a store. Have you ever lost a receipt that you needed? Do all stores give cash refunds? People who lose their receipts must be mad when they can't return something to a store. Do you know anyone who couldn't return something because they had lost the receipt?

Understanding Pie Charts

Earl used the Internet to learn more about the lemon law in his state. Of course, because so many people are buying and selling things on the Internet, consumers sometimes have problems. In fact, Internet fraud is fast becoming a major problem. In 2000, people lost over $3 million to Internet fraud.

With a partner, look at the information about Internet fraud:

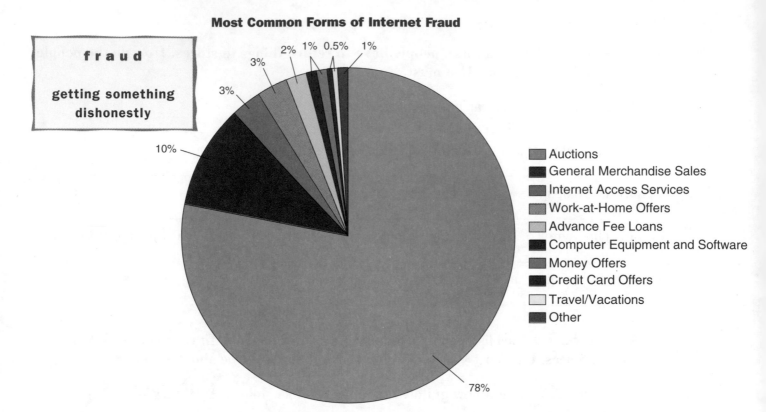

Most Common Forms of Internet Fraud

fraud

getting something
dishonestly

- Auctions
- General Merchandise Sales
- Internet Access Services
- Work-at-Home Offers
- Advance Fee Loans
- Computer Equipment and Software
- Money Offers
- Credit Card Offers
- Travel/Vacations
- Other

Exercise 12 Earl was surprised at what he learned about fraud. In your notebook, answer the questions about the information.

1. How much money did people lose to Internet fraud in 2000?
2. What was the average loss?
3. What kind of fraud is the most common on the Internet?
4. Did many people lose money on fraud related to computer equipment?
5. Did more people lose money from buying merchandise or from credit card offers?
6. What is the least common form of Internet fraud?
7. How can you lose money from an advance-fee loan on the Internet?
8. How can you lose money when buying merchandise on the Internet?

Talk About It

In a group, talk about a consumer problem you or someone you know has experienced. It could be fraud, or some other kind of problem such as buying a lemon. What did you do about the problem? Tell your group. Listen to what the people in your group did about their problems. Make a pie chart to show the different kinds of consumer problems. What is the most common consumer problem in your group? Share your group's experiences with the class.

Issues and Answers

Earl wrote to Ms. Moneybags. Read the letter and Ms. Moneybags' advice. Then talk with other students about the advice. Do you agree? What other advice can you give?

 *Ask Ms. Moneybags*

DEAR MS. MONEYBAGS,

I am upset because the new computer game I bought for my son doesn't work. I bought the game on the Internet. We tried to return it but the company won't take the game back. Every time we try to play it there is a new problem. I think that I should get my money back, but so far the company has not listened to me. This must be some kind of fraud, and I want to know how to get a refund for this game.

—UPSET GAME OWNER

DEAR UPSET,

You must be mad about the game. Luckily, there may be help for you. The Better Business Bureau helps people who have problems with companies. Sometimes the consumer can get his or her money back. To get help from the Better Business Bureau, just call them. If they can't fix the problem then you may get a refund or a new game. The decision is up to the company. The laws are different in each state, so check with your Better Business Bureau to find out the exact rules. Then talk to the company again and say you want the Better Business Bureau to help solve the problem.

Sincerely,

—MS. MONEYBAGS

 Your Turn

Upset Game Owner needs information about consumer protection laws in his state.

Step 1:   Look at the pie chart on page 94. What kind of fraud did Upset Game Owner experience?

Step 2:   With your partner, look in the telephone book under "Consumer Groups." Make a list of places you can call to help solve consumer problems. You can also use the Internet to find out the information.

Step 3:   Share the information you found with the class.

Community Involvement

Before you make a major purchase, find out about the product you are going to buy. Magazines such as *Consumer Reports* have articles about major purchases such as cars, appliances, vacation packages, and so on. You can use this information to help you make the best choice. Second, find out about the store where you will make the purchase. Make sure that the store has a good reputation.

Your Turn

With a partner, think of a major purchase you want to make. Are you thinking of buying a car, an air conditioner, or a TV? Have you bought one before in the United States? Did you make any major purchases in your native country? Where did you look for information before you made your purchase?

Community Action

Step 1: With a partner, think of information you need in order to make the major purchase above. Which brands do you know? Which store has the best reputation? What is the store's return policy? Write the information in your notebook.

Step 2: Make a list of sources of information about the product you want to buy. Look in the library for magazines, the Internet for consumer information web sites on this product, and the telephone directory for consumer groups such as the Better Business Bureau. Find the answers to these questions. Write the information in your notebook.
- Which magazines have consumer information?
- Do these magazines have a good reputation?
- What web sites give consumer information?
- What is the best web site you found?
- Are there phone numbers for local consumer groups in your city?
- Write down the group names and phone numbers.

 ## Talk About It

In a group, talk about the consumer information you found. Where can you find information about specific products and services? Which sources were the most help? Why? Share your ideas with the class.

Wrap Up

Now Marge and Earl have a new car that runs well. There are many ways to solve a problem with a purchase. Work with a partner. In your notebook, make an idea map like the one below. Fill in your idea map with ways that consumers can protect their rights.

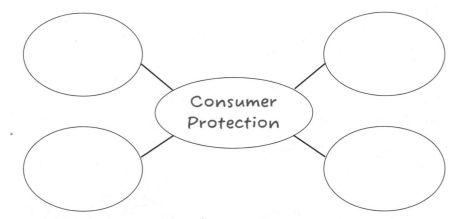

With a partner, role-play a conversation about a purchase you made. You want to return it, and your partner gives you advice. Use **have to, should, must, must not, don't have to,** and **must** for probability. Use your ideas above and words from this unit. For example:

   A: I just bought a new VCR, but it doesn't work. It must be broken.
   B: That's too bad. You must be angry. You should take it back.
   A: Well, I lost the receipt. You have to have a receipt to take it back.
   B: Have you checked your car? Maybe it's there.
   A: That's a good idea. Let's look now. My car is right outside.
   B: You should always keep your receipts so you can get a refund.

Practice your role-play. Then share it with the class.

Think About Learning

Check (✔) to show your learning in this unit. Write one more thing at the bottom.

SKILLS / STRUCTURES	PAGE	EASY 😊	SO-SO 😐	DIFFICULT 😟
Talk about returning something to a store	86, 90			
Understand conversations about consumer rights and return policies	87, 91			
Use **should** and **have to**	88			
Read about the Better Business Bureau	89			
Use **must, must not,** and **don't have to**	92			
Use **must** to show probability	93			
Read and create a pie chart to express ideas	94			
Find consumer information in your community	95			
Learn how to research a major purchase	96			

unit 9   The Local Park District

 Scene 1: Conversation

Read the scene with a partner. Listen to the conversation and practice it together.

Rhonda is talking to her friend Zanta about her daycare problems.

 Ask your partner the questions below. Then share your answers with another pair or with the class.

Facts	What is the problem? What are Rhonda and Zanta talking about?
Feelings	How does Rhonda feel? Why?
And You	Do you need a service like the After School Program? Why?
Comparisons	What do kids do after school in your native country?

Your Turn

98   Now write or tell the story in your own words.

Vocabulary

Look at the pictures and read the words below with a partner. Talk about what the words mean. Look up the words in a dictionary and write the meanings in your notebook.

snack

scout

weight room

park district
volunteer
to bother
to bring (something) up

Your Words

_____

_____

Exercise 1 Rhonda is worried about where her children can go after school. Match the words in Column A with the definitions in Column B. Write the letter.

COLUMN A	COLUMN B
_____ 1. park district	**a.** it's responsible for the parks
_____ 2. Girl Scout	**b.** someone who works for free
_____ 3. volunteer	**c.** a girl who is a member of this organization for girls
_____ 4. to bother	**d.** to start talking about that subject
_____ 5. to bring up an idea	**e.** to upset someone

Listening

Before You Listen Look at the pictures and read the phrases. What advice would you give to each person?

Exercise 2 Different people in the neighborhood have different problems. Listen to the conversations. Circle the letter of the phrase that best describes the solution to each problem.

1.

Mrs. Robinson should
a. Organize a neighborhood clean-up day.
b. Call the park district office and complain.
c. Call the police.

2.

Mr. Gomez should
a. Call Homework Hotline.
b. Call his son's teacher.
c. Call the park district.

3.

Yolanda's son should
a. join the Boy Scouts.
b. become a volunteer.
c. go to the public library.

4.
The park district should
a. clean up the park.
b. have more activities.
c. put out more trash cans.

After You Listen With a partner, compare your answers. Was your advice correct?

Your Turn

With a partner, talk about where you want to volunteer. Where will you help? Will you be a Boy Scout leader? a Meals on Wheels volunteer? Share your partner's answer with the class.

SPOTLIGHT on *Used To*

I **used to** play basketball at Gill Park. Now I go swimming at Gill Park.
He **used to** volunteer with the Boy Scouts. Now he volunteers at the park district.
It **used to** be open on Sunday.
They **used to** bother the people in the park.

Use **used to** to talk about things done in the past, but not done now.

Did you use to play basketball in Gill Park?   Yes, I **did**./No, I **didn't**.
Did they use to eat a snack before playing in the park?

Use **did (you) use to** to ask questions.

Exercise 3 Zanta used to keep her children at home after school, but now they go to the After School Program. Rewrite the sentences. Use <u>used to</u> and <u>use to</u>.

1. Rhonda's mother took care of Rhonda's kids. Now they go to the After School Program.
   Rhonda's mother used to take care of Rhonda's kids.

2. Frank swam at Gill Park Pool. Now he swims at Oak Street Beach.
   _____

3. Marion exercised in the weight room. Now she exercises in the pool.
   _____

4. Did she study Spanish at City Community College? She doesn't study Spanish now.
   _____

5. I belonged to a book club. Now I belong to a hiking club.
   _____

6. Did they play basketball at the gym every day? They only play on weekends now.
   _____

Exercise 4 In your notebook, write five sentences about things you used to do as a child, and what you do now. Use <u>used to</u>. For example, write "I used to go to school. Now I take my kids to school."

 Pair Work

Listen to the conversation between Rhonda and Zanta. Then practice it with a partner.

Rhonda: I read the brochure about the After School Program. I'll get more information from the office tomorrow. It's a good program. But our parents never worried about us. We used to play outside until it was dark.

Zanta: You're right, but things were different then. Your kids will love the Gill Park program. My mother used to watch my kids too. Now she volunteers at the park district.

 In Your Experience

In your notebook, write sentences about what you and your partner used to do when you were children. Use the sentences from Exercise 4 to help you. For example, write "I used to play at the park. José used to play at the beach."

Reading for Real

Rhonda is reading a brochure Zanta gave her about the programs at Gill Park.

GILL PARK AND COMMUNITY CENTER
Fun for the whole family

Everyone in your family can have a good time—whether they're a young child, a teenager, an adult, or a senior!

SWIMMING

Water Exercise Class for Seniors
  Monday to Friday 10:00 to 11:00 a.m.

Free Swim
  Monday to Saturday 6:00 to 8:30 p.m.

AFTER SCHOOL PROGRAM

For children from kindergarten to fifth grade. After school, kids can study, use the gym, get a snack, or get help with their homework.

  Monday to Friday 2:30 to 6:30

BASKETBALL FOR TEENS

Up to four games can take place at the same time.

  Open • Monday to Friday: 6:30
       to midnight
  Gym • Saturday: 8:00 to midnight

WEIGHT ROOM

  Monday to Saturday
    6:00 a.m. to 8:30 p.m.

MEETING ROOMS

The rooms at our community center are available for community meetings, every day from 2:00 p.m. to 9:00 p.m. Use of the rooms is free but must be reserved in advance.

  Groups using the rooms include:
    Afternoon Sewing Circle
    Single Parents' Club
    Boy Scouts
    Cancer Survivors' Support Group
    Hispanic Neighbors' Association
    Girl Scouts

Exercise 5 Many community centers offer different programs. Read the brochure again. Write the name of the program or facility that will help each person.

1. Katrina wants to make sure her young children are safe while she is at work.
   _____

2. Virginia is new in town and wants to make friends. She loves to make her own clothes. _____

3. Mrs. Russo is 65 years old. Her doctor told her to lose weight and get more exercise._____

4. Donna Lee has three kids. Her husband died two years ago.
   _____

5. Amanda's book club used to meet at a restaurant, but that's too expensive.
   _____

6. Ricardo wants to have more muscle so he can play football next year.
   _____

Talk About It

In a group, talk about the activities at Gill Park. Are you interested in any of the activities? Which ones? What other activities could the park offer? Share your ideas with your partner. Tell your partner's ideas to the class.

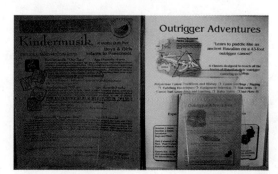

Read the scene with a partner. Listen to the conversation and practice it together.

Rhonda is signing her children up for the After School Program at the park office.

Facts	What is the clerk talking about?
Feelings	How does Rhonda feel? Why?
And You	Would you use the After School Program for your kids? Why?
Comparisons	Do park districts in your native country have activities for families?

Your Turn

Now write or tell the story in your own words.

Vocabulary

Look at the words below with a partner. Talk about what the words mean. Look up the words in a dictionary and write the meanings in your notebook.

available
ideal
organization

to have (something) in mind
to participate

Exercise 6 It is important to get information about the services in your community. Complete the sentences. Write the correct word on the line. Use the words above to help you.

1. The Boy Scouts is an _____ for boys to enjoy themselves outdoors.

2. Rhonda _____ for her kids to do after school.

3. Ana cooks delicious food. Meals on Wheels is _____ for her.

4. We need someone to help at the After School Program. Are you _____ after school from 3:00 to 6:00?

5. Mrs. Sanchez _____ in the Afternoon Sewing Circle every week.

 # Listening

Before You Listen Read about the volunteer programs and the people listed below. Who do you think will volunteer for each of the Our City Cares programs?

Exercise 7 Some people are calling to volunteer at Our City Cares. Listen and decide which program they should help. Write the letter of the program on the line.

OUR CITY CARES VOLUNTEER PROGRAMS

a. **Meals on Wheels** Prepare and deliver meals to seniors.

b. **Coats for Kids** This program gives old winter coats to children who need them.

c. **Homework Hotline** Kids call for help with their homework. Our volunteers are teachers and adults with college degrees. They can answer your child's questions.

d. **Business Technology Classes** Help adults learn to use computers, cash registers, and other business machines.

e. **Community Helpers** Help seniors with big and small chores. Our volunteers drive seniors to the doctor, help them at the supermarket, and perform small tasks around their homes.

_____ 1. Mr. Green

_____ 2. Mrs. Vasquez

_____ 3. Mr. Jones

_____ 4. Ms. Williams

_____ 5. Ms. Hirsch

After You Listen With a partner, compare your answers. Were your predictions correct?

 Your Turn

With a partner, talk about programs in your community. Where do you want to volunteer? Why? Share your partner's ideas with the class.

SPOTLIGHT on the Past Perfect

Simple Past   Past Perfect

Before she **called** Our City Cares, she **had decided** to become a volunteer.

action that happened later - - - > action that happened earliest

She decided to become a volunteer.

She called "Our City Cares."   NOW
Past

They **had called** the park district before they **organized** the clean-up day.

action that happened earliest - - - > action that happened later

We bought some trash bags.

We cleaned the park.   NOW
Past

We **cleaned** the park after we **had bought** some trash bags at the supermarket.

action that happened later - - - > action that happened earliest

Past perfect is **had + past participle.** For a list of common past participles, see page 122. Use the past perfect to talk about a past action that happened before another past action. The action that happened earliest is in the past perfect. The action that happened later is in the simple past.

Exercise 8 Rhonda thought about the park programs after her mother had told her she couldn't watch the children. Complete the sentences. Use the past perfect and the simple past.

1. Zanta _____had told_____ (tell) Rhonda about the After School Program before

   Rhonda _____went_____ (go) to the park office.

2. Before their grandmother _____ (find) a new job, Rhonda's kids

   _____ (stay) at their grandmother's house after school.

3. After Rhonda's kids _____ (visit) the program, they

   _____ (be) excited.

4. Rhonda _____ (be) worried about her kids, but the After School

   Program _____ (help) her feel better.

Exercise 9 In your notebook, write a few sentences about things you had done before you came to the United States. Use the past perfect. Use the Exercise 8 as a model. For example, write "Before I came to the United States, I had decided to go to school."

Talk About It

In a group, talk about what you had done before you arrived in the United States. Use your information in Exercise 9 to ask and answer questions. For example, ask "Had you studied English before you came to the United States?" Share your answers with the class.

SPOTLIGHT on the Past Perfect Progressive

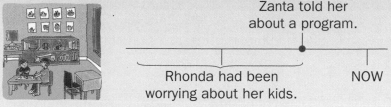

Past Action   Another Past Action

Rhonda **had been worrying** about her kids before Zanta **told** her about a program.

Zanta told her
about a program.

Rhonda had been
worrying about her kids.   NOW

Use the past perfect progressive to talk about a past action that continued over time in the past but ended before another past action.

Before Zanta told her about a program, Rhonda **had worried** about her kids.
The past perfect or the past perfect progressive with the same meaning is often used. Use the past perfect continuous to give emphasis to the fact that the action happened over time.

Exercise 10 Many people volunteer for community groups. Complete the sentences. Use the correct form of the verb in the simple past or past perfect progressive.

1. He ___had been living___ (live) in Chicago for five years when he ___moved___ (move) to Texas.

2. Brent _____ (volunteer) at the public library when he _____ (decide) to volunteer at Homework Hotline.

3. Rhonda _____ (talk) to Zanta when she _____ (find) out about the After School Program.

4. Tyrone _____ (get) ready for work when the phone _____ (ring).

5. Before I _____ (become) a volunteer at the After School Program, I _____ (feel) sad and lonely.

Exercise 11 In your notebook, write a few sentences imagining that you were busy at home when the phone rang. What had you been doing when the phone rang?

 Pair Work

Listen to the conversation between Rhonda and Zanta. Then practice it with a partner.

Rhonda: My children love the After School Program at the park district. All they had been doing was watching TV before they went to Gill Park.

Zanta: My children used to watch a lot of TV too.

Rhonda: Every night, one of my kids brings up park programs they want to join.

Zanta: There is a swimming class in October. Maybe our kids can join together.

Rhonda: I had decided to sign them up for swimming lessons before. It will be good to have them in the same class.

 Your Turn

With a partner, talk about the sentences you wrote in Exercise 11. What had your partner been doing when the phone rang? Use the information you wrote for Exercise 11. Share your partner's answers with the class.

Understanding Bar Graphs

Rhonda read in the newspaper about a group of volunteers in New York City. New York Cares is a community organization that helps people in New York. In New York Cares, volunteers help on many long-term and short-term projects, including Clean-Up Days, computer classes, and more. Here are some numbers that show the success of New York Cares.

On New York Cares Day, volunteers painted classrooms and playgrounds, organized libraries, and did other work in 100 public schools.

On Spring Clean-Up Day, volunteers provided over 20,000 hours of service to clean up and care for the city's parks.

After September 11, 2001, New York Cares volunteers provided 35,000 hours of disaster volunteer service in less than four months.

Look at the bar graph. It shows the number of volunteers who worked on three projects:

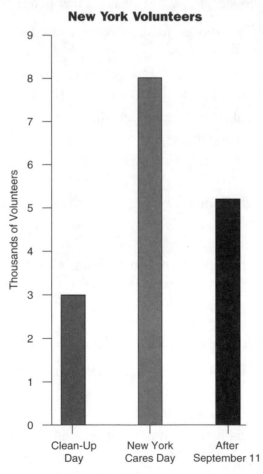

New York Volunteers

(y-axis: Thousands of Volunteers, 0 to 9)
(x-axis: Clean-Up Day, New York Cares Day, After September 11)

Exercise 12 The volunteers at New York Cares did a lot of things to help the community. In your notebook, answer the questions about the information and the graph.

1. What is New York Cares?
2. Where did volunteers work on New York Cares Day?
3. Where did volunteers work on Spring Clean-up Day?
4. Did New York Cares volunteers give a lot of help after September 11? Why do you think so?
5. Which project had the most volunteers?
6. Which project had the fewest volunteers?
7. Which of the projects on the bar graph would you like to help? Why?
8. Is New York Cares a good organization? Why do you think so?

Talk About It

In a group, talk about the different ways people in your group volunteer. Find the hours that each student in your group helped others. Then use the total hours to make a bar graph. Show your class the graph and tell the class about some of the people that students in your group helped. Then use the information from all of the groups to make a class graph. What is the total number of hours your class helped others?

Issues and Answers

Zanta's new neighbor wrote to Abdul and Anita. Read the letter and Abdul's advice. Then talk with other students about the advice. Do you agree? What other advice can you give?

Ask Abdul and Anita

DEAR ABDUL AND ANITA,

I just moved to town, and I feel very sad and lonely. I volunteered a lot in my old town, and that kept me busy. So I want to start volunteering here, but I want to pick a project that will help the town. I speak Spanish and English, have a car, and know how to use a computer. I don't know where to call to get information about volunteer organizations in my new town. Please help me find a place to volunteer.

Signed,

—WANTS TO VOLUNTEER

DEAR VOLUNTEER,

There are lots of ways to volunteer in any town. The park district is an organization that always needs volunteer help. They need people to teach classes, help with after school activities, and supervise playgrounds. You can also call charitable organizations such as the historic society and hospitals and find out the projects they are working on. Then choose the one that interests you the most. They always need people to volunteer. You have great skills, so many organizations will want your help. Good luck!

Respectfully,

—ABDUL

 Your Turn

Wants to Volunteer wants to join an organization in town in order to make friends and have fun.

Step 1: With your partner, list places where "Wants to Volunteer" can help. If you need ideas, call the Park District or the United Way to get a list of charities, or look them up on the Internet.

Step 2: Pick one of the organizations that interests you. Find out more information about how to volunteer.

Step 3: Share the information you found with the class. What kinds of activities does the organization offer? Will "Wants to Volunteer" be able to help there? Would you like to be a part of the organization? Why? Why not?

Community Involvement

Park districts are great community organizations. Park districts offer exercise, activities, and a lot of organizations. What services does the park district in your city or town offer? Which services do you want to use? Which services do you want your children to use?

Your Turn

With a partner, talk about parks in your native countries. Are they the same or different from parks in the United States? Why? Do the park districts there have services for families? What kind of activities are there? Are they expensive? Share your answers with the class.

Community Action

Step 1: With a partner, make a list in your notebook of services you think park districts should offer to the community. Include sports, clubs, organizations, and activities. Choose three important services from your list. They can be important to you, your friends, or your family.

Step 2: Get a brochure from your local park district, or use the Internet to find information about the services you chose in Step 1. Find the answers to these questions. Write the answers in your notebook.
  · What services does your local park district offer?
  · Do they offer any of the top three services on your list? Which ones?
  · How much do the services cost?
  · Are the services different for each season?

 ## Talk About It

In a group, talk about the information you found on your local park district. Which activities interest you? Which ones interest your classmates? Will you volunteer to help? Do you plan to participate in any of the activities?

Wrap Up

Rhonda found some wonderful programs for herself and her children at Gill Park. How can your park district help you? Complete the T-chart in your notebook. Think of at least three things that you want to do.

What you want to do	Solution
I need more exercise.	Swim at the park district pool.

With a partner, role-play a conversation. One person is lonely, or their kids need some after-school activities. The other person offers advice. Use the past perfect, past perfect progressive, and **used to.** Use words from this unit. For example:

A: I'm worried about my kids. They haven't been making many friends or participating in activities outside of school. They used to have lots to do before we moved.

B: Really? Did you know that the park district offers activities for children?

A: I had thought of calling the park district when we first moved in, but I was too busy.

B: Well, there's a theater group for kids. And kids can take swimming lessons in the evenings.

A: That's great. How can I find out more information?

B: Just go to any park office and ask for a brochure. Or check the Internet.

Practice your role-play. Then share it with the class.

Think About Learning

Check (✔) to show your learning in this unit. Write one more thing at the bottom.

SKILLS / STRUCTURES	PAGE	EASY 😊	SO-SO 😐	DIFFICULT 😞
Talk about services at the park district	98, 102			
Understand conversations about community organizations	99, 103			
Use **used to**	100			
Read a recreation schedule	101			
Use the past perfect	104			
Use the past perfect progressive	105			
Read and create a bar graph to express ideas	106			
Find out about volunteer opportunities in your community	107			
Learn about park district services in your community	108			

unit 10 Body Language

 Scene 1: Conversation

Read the scene with a partner. Listen to the conversation and practice it together.

Mike and Bev are in Bev's office. She is the manager of the bank.

 Ask your partner the questions below. Then share your answers with another pair or with the class.

Facts	What's the problem? How can Tina solve it?
Feelings	How does Tina feel? How do you know? How does Mike feel? Why?
And You?	Has something like this ever happened to you? What did you do?
Comparisons	How do people greet one another in your native country?

Your Turn

Now write or tell the story in your own words.

Vocabulary

Look at the pictures and read the words below with a partner. Talk about what the words mean. Look up the words in a dictionary and write the meanings in your notebook.

Your Words

_____

_____

to grin from   to shake   to stare   eye contact
ear to ear   hands   into space

firm   polite   to have (my) hands full   to refuse
head (teller)   to get (your) hands dirty   to keep on

Exercise 1 Tina needs to learn about body language. Match the pictures in Column A with the phrases in Column B. Use the words above to help you. The pictures could be used more than once. Write the letter.

COLUMN A

a.

b.

c.

d.

COLUMN B

_____ 1. to shake hands

_____ 2. have (my) hands full

_____ 3. eye contact

_____ 4. get (your) hands dirty

_____ 5. polite

Listening

Before You Listen Read the phrases below. What problems are the people having?

Exercise 2 Listen to the conversations about people's jobs. Circle the letter of the phrase that best completes each sentence.

1. Chin enjoys working
   a. at Accurate Accounting.
   b. as an accountant.
   c. with people.

2. Jeffrey should keep on
   a. painting.
   b. staring into space.
   c. worrying about his son.

3. Amy quit working as a hair stylist because she
   a. dislikes getting her hands dirty.
   b. enjoys working with computers.
   c. got an allergy to chemicals.

4. Now Chin is thinking about
   a. buying a home.
   b. getting a job.
   c. moving to another city.

After You Listen With a partner, compare your answers. Did you find the correct problems?

Your Turn

With a partner, talk about the kind of work you like to do. Do you like to be active? Do you like to work in an office?

SPOTLIGHT on Gerunds

I enjoy **working** outside.
He needs to stop **running** in the sun.
We have to keep on **building** until we finish the job.
Will they talk about **changing** the new contract?

Gardening is hard work.
Using correct body language is important.

A gerund is the **-ing** form of the verb. It acts like a noun.

A gerund can also be the subject of a sentence.

All of these verbs can be followed by a gerund: enjoy, keep on, hate, stop, finish, talk about, miss, quit, think about, dislike, recommend

Exercise 3 Bev and Mike are eating lunch in the break room. Tina is greeting them. Read the conversation. Write the correct word on the line. Use gerunds.

| do | garden | get | see | weed | work |

Tina: Hi Bev. Hi Mike. Mike, how do you like **(1)** ___working___ here?

Mike: I like it. I especially like the hours. This job gives me more time to do things I like. But I do miss **(2)** _____ all my old friends.

Tina: What do you like to do, Mike?

Mike: I really enjoy **(3)** _____.

Tina: Do you? I like planting, but I hate **(4)** _____. That's the worst part of gardening.

Bev: Well, I like gardens as much as you, but I hate **(5)** _____ the work. I don't like **(6)** _____ my hands dirty.

Exercise 4 In your notebook, write about a job you used to have. Complete the sentences using gerunds. For example, write "I was a waiter. I enjoyed talking to people in restaurants."

I was a/an . . .   I miss . . .
I enjoyed . . .   I disliked . . .

 Pair Work

Listen to the conversation between Tina and Bev. Then practice it with a partner.

Tina: Thank you for introducing me to Mike. He's a very polite person.
Bev: He will be good for the bank. He will be changing some things.
Tina: What will he be changing?
Bev: Mike is thinking about hiring new employees.
Tina: That would be good. We need more help.
Bev: He will be recommending that at the next staff meeting.

 Your Turn

With a partner, ask and answer questions about your old jobs. Use the information from Exercise 4 to help you. Use gerunds like **living, moving, having,** and **feeling.** Use **think about, miss, dislike, like, enjoy.** Share your answers with the class.

Reading for Real

Tina read a magazine article about shaking hands in America.

to squeeze

Shaking Hands, American Style

People often shake hands in the United States. American men shake hands with other men. American women often shake hands with men, and sometimes they shake hands with other women. Adults shake hands with children. And some people even teach their dogs to shake hands! How do people shake hands correctly? How do they shake hands just long enough? just hard enough? Here are five little rules to remember:

1. Use your right hand.
2. Use good eye contact. Look at the person in the eye while you are shaking hands.
3. Don't shake too long. Shake for no more than three seconds. Then let go and pull your hand back toward you.
4. Don't squeeze too strongly or too weakly. When a handshake is weak, Americans think the person may not be a hard worker or a good leader. When a handshake is too strong, Americans think the person is too rough or has bad manners.
5. Don't relax your wrist too much. Move your arm up and down at the elbow, but move your wrist just a little.

When do people in the United States shake hands? They shake hands when they meet for the first time. They shake hands to say congratulations. They shake hands when they meet after not seeing each other for a while. And they often shake hands when they say good-bye. In business, shaking hands shows agreement and honesty. But the meaning of shaking hands is most important when people do not do it. It is not polite to refuse a person's hand.

Exercise 5 Tina is thinking about the article she read. What did Tina learn about body language? Read the article again. Write <u>yes</u> or <u>no</u> on the line.

_____ 1. Shaking hands is a very common greeting.

_____ 2. You should use your right hand to shake hands.

_____ 3. When you shake hands, shake the hand for three minutes to show you're happy to meet the person.

_____ 4. Always maintain good eye contact when shaking hands.

_____ 5. It's a bad idea to squeeze very weakly.

_____ 6. It's OK to refuse to shake someone's hand.

Talk About It

In a group, talk about greetings in your native country. Do people shake hands? If so, do they shake hands the same way that Americans do? If they don't shake hands, how do people greet one another? What should Americans do when they visit your native country?

Read the scene with a partner. Listen to the conversation and practice it together.

Tina is getting ready to apply for a promotion at the bank. She's talking to a job counselor to get ready for the interviews.

An important part of applying for a job is your body language. Your body language needs to give a good impression.

Yes, I have trouble using the right body language. You see, I'm from Colombia, and our body language is different.

Well, rules for shaking hands, eye contact, and posture are all important. When you shake hands, shake hands firmly but not too hard.

Sometimes people feel uncomfortable when I shake their hand.

You shouldn't continue shaking their hand for a long time. Continue to shake for only three seconds. Just count one-two-three as you shake. Then let go. Remember to use good posture too. Stand up straight, and don't slump in your chair.

Oh, yes. Good posture is important everywhere, I think. Thanks for the advice.

 Ask your partner the questions below. Then share your answers with another pair or with the class.

Facts	What's the problem? How can the counselor help Tina?
Feelings	How does Tina feel?
And You?	What do you do to get ready for a job interview?
Comparisons	How do people in your native country act when they apply for new jobs?

Your Turn

Now write or tell the story in your own words.

Vocabulary

Look at the pictures and read the words below with a partner. Talk about what the words mean. Look up the words in a dictionary and write the meanings in your notebook.

good posture

bad posture

comfortable

uncomfortable

to slump

impression
body language
to hold up (your) head
to shake on it

Exercise 6 How you look and act at a job interview is important. Complete the sentences. Write the correct word on the line. Use the words above to help you.

1. _____ shows that you take pride in yourself.

2. I am very glad that you are taking this job. Let's _____ on it.

3. Don't _____ in your chair like that. It's terrible for your back.

4. Sit in this chair. It's really _____.

5. To have good posture, you need to _____ your head.

6. To leave a good _____ at a job interview, wear nice clothes.

 # Listening

Before You Listen Tina is still talking to the job counselor. Read the sentences. What do you think they're talking about?

Exercise 7 Do you know how to interview for a job? Listen to the conversation and write <u>yes</u> or <u>no</u> on the line.

_____ 1. You shouldn't squeeze the person's hand too hard.

_____ 2. You shouldn't shake hands at the end of the interview.

_____ 3. When you reach an important agreement, you should "shake on it."

_____ 4. For good eye contact, don't look the other person in the eyes.

_____ 5. Always stand up straight and hold up your head.

After You Listen With a partner, compare your answers. Do you understand good body language?

Your Turn

With a partner, talk about going to a job interview. Your partner is getting ready for a job interview. He or she wants to make a good impression. Take turns asking for and giving advice.

SPOTLIGHT on Infinitives

I want **to go** to the supermarket.
He needs **to go** to a meeting.
They plan **to find** new jobs next year.

He agreed **to take** the job.
She is offering **to help** us.
The manager decided **to promote** Tina.

What did you choose **to do,** Mark?
Did she refuse **to shake** your hand?

An infinitive is the **to** form of a verb.

An infinitive can be the object of a verb.

All of these verbs can be followed by an infinitive: agree, ask, choose, decide, hope, learn, need, offer, refuse, seem, volunteer, want

Exercise 8 Tina decided to apply for a promotion. Complete the sentences. Write the correct word on the line. Use the infinitive form.

find	get	learn	stay	teach	use

1. Tina decided _____ to find _____ a new job.

2. Tina went to the job counselor because she wants _____ good job search skills.

3. The counselor offered _____ her good body language skills.

4. Tina hopes _____ her skills to give a good impression during the interview.

5. She wants _____ promoted to manager.

6. Tina doesn't want _____ head teller forever.

Exercise 9 In your notebook, write a few sentences about a new job you want to find. Write about the things you need to do and the body language you need to use when you look for a job. Use verbs such as <u>decide</u>, <u>need</u>, <u>volunteer</u>, <u>learn</u>, <u>refuse</u>, plus infinitives.

Talk About It

In a group, talk about your job search. Use the information you gathered in Exercise 9. Then share your story with the class.

SPOTLIGHT on Gerunds and Infinitives

They volunteered **to help** at the Senior Center. She refuses **to maintain** good eye contact.	Some verbs can be followed only by infinitives.
He quit **working** there two years ago. She likes **shaking** hands with customers.	Some verbs can be followed only by gerunds.

Some verbs, such as those below, can be followed by either gerunds or infinitives.

begin	can stand	continue	use	forget	hate
like	talk	love	start	stop	try

He continued **talking**. He continued **to talk**.	They tried **to use** good body language. They tried **using** good body language.

Exercise 10 Tina's friend wants to find a better paying job too. Complete the sentences. Write the correct word on the line. Use a gerund or an infinitive.

1. I love <u>reading or to read</u> (**read**) about cultural differences.

2. I know how _____ (**shake**) hands appropriately.

3. I also started _____ (**maintain**) good posture.

4. However, I refuse _____ (**give up**) some customs from my country.

5. I am from Morocco. In my country people like _____ (**touch**) their hearts after they shake hands.

6. I will always continue _____ (**use**) this Moroccan custom when I shake hands.

Exercise 11 In your notebook, write about your job and the job you want. Complete the sentences. Use verbs plus a gerund or an infinitive.

I love . . .	I recommend . . .	I need . . .
I enjoy . . .	I miss . . .	

Pair Work

Listen to the conversation between Tina and Mike. Then practice it with a partner.

Tina: I have to go to a job interview tomorrow for my promotion.

Mike: Do you want me to help you get ready? We could practice some interview questions.

Tina: It would be good to practice. Do you have time now?

Mike: Yes. You should start by using good body language.

Your Turn

With a partner, talk about your ideal job. Use verbs plus gerunds or infinitives. For example, say "I like to talk with people at work. I like helping customers find clothes."

Understanding Pie Charts

When we talk, words are not the only tools we use. Our bodies talk too. Speaking with words is called verbal language. Speaking with our bodies is called nonverbal language, or body language. The way we move our hands, our bodies, and our eyes all show our thoughts.

tone the emotion in your voice
s p e e d how fast you speak
i n t o n a t i o n the music in your voice
v o l u m e how loud you speak

Most people actually speak words for only about 10 minutes a day. The average sentence takes only about 2.5 seconds to say. In a conversation, only a tiny part of the communication is verbal. The rest is nonverbal (body language) and vocal (tone, speed, volume, and so on). Look at the pie chart. The pie chart shows the three ways we send messages to people.

Exercise 1 2 Tina has learned a lot about the body language to use in an interview and at work. In your notebook, answer the following questions.

Types of Communication

- 38% vocal (voice)
- 7% verbal
- 55% nonverbal

1. What nonverbal communication shows our thoughts?
2. Name three parts of vocal expression. Explain how they work.
3. Name two nonverbal expressions. What do they mean in the United States or your native country?
4. How long does a person speak each day?
5. How much time is needed to say a sentence?
6. What is the percentage of nonverbal communication?
7. What is the percentage of verbal communication?

8. Which is more important, verbal, vocal, or nonverbal communication? Why do you think so?

Talk About It

In a group, role-play a job interview. Two students will perform the interview. Make sure you include verbal, vocal, and nonverbal communication. The other members of the group will time the number of seconds each person spoke. Then the students will perform the conversation again and the other students will take notes on the conversation. In your notebook, write the verbal message, the nonverbal message, and vocal message.

Review the information. What percentage of the communication was verbal? vocal? nonverbal? Make a pie chart. Share your pie chart with the class.

1. Verbal _____%
2. Vocal (tone, speed, and so on) _____%
3. Nonverbal (body language) _____%

Issues and Answers

Tina wrote to Mr. Nakamura to ask about body language. Read the letter and Mr. Nakamura's advice. Then talk with other students about the advice. Do you agree? What other advice can you give?

 Ask Mr. Nakamura

DEAR MR. NAKAMURA,

I have been working at an American company for a year. I really enjoy my job, and my coworkers are very nice. But sometimes when I am speaking to them, they move away from me. Am I offending them? I'm from Latin America. I want to correct this problem because I'll be getting a promotion soon.

—FRIENDLY WORKER

DEAR FRIENDLY WORKER,

American body space is different from the space you probably are comfortable with in your native country. Americans usually like about two feet of space around them when they talk to someone. This is a comfortable body space in the United States. Keep talking to your friends, but give them a little more space! As for your promotion, there are plenty of good books that give advice on preparing for interviews, including body language.

Sincerely,

—MR. NAKAMURA,
HUMAN RESOURCES MANAGER

 ## Your Turn

Friendly Worker needs to improve her body language to get ready for a new job.

Step 1: With a partner, list problems with body language, such as slumping.

Step 2: Write a list of instructions for Friendly Worker. Use the information about verbal, nonverbal, and vocal communication on page 118 to help you. For example, write "She shouldn't stand close to people. Standing too close makes people feel uncomfortable."

Step 3: Share the information you gathered with the class. Which group had the best advice?

Community Involvement

Because body language communicates a lot of information, it's very helpful to understand it. Everyone's body language is different in formal and informal situations.

Your Turn

With a partner, think of your body language at work and at home in your native country. Describe the body language you use in each situation. Do you think it is the same all the time, or different sometimes? Why?

Community Action

Step 1: With a partner, talk about American body language at work and at home. Is it the same as in your native country? How do you think it is different? Write the answers in your notebook.

Step 2: With a partner, observe Americans at work and in a relaxed situation, such as shopping or at the park. Watch the people's body language. What's the same? What's different? Where do people use more body language? Write what you see in your notebook.

Talk About It

In a group, share the information you found about American body language. What are the differences between formal and informal American body language? Which group found the most differences between work body language and relaxed body language? Share your information with the class. Use the information from your class to prepare a class booklet on body language in the United States.

Wrap Up

How well do you know American body language? In a group, make a T-chart like the one below about body language in a job interview. What should you do to send the right messages?

Part of the Body	What You Should Do
Eyes	
Handshake	
Posture	
Other	

With a partner, role-play a conversation about a job interview. One person wants advice about body language. The other person gives the advice. Use gerunds, infinitives, and words from this unit. For example:

A: I'm really nervous about my job interview.

B: Don't worry. I'm sure you'll get the job. Don't forget to shake hands firmly.

A: I'll remember that. What else should I do?

B: Well, wearing nice clothes is important. And, looking the interviewer in the eye is important too.

A: Thanks. That's good advice.

B: I'm sure you will be working soon.

Practice your role-play. Then share it with the class.

Think About Learning

Check (✔) to show your learning in this unit. Write one more thing at the bottom.

SKILLS / STRUCTURES	PAGE	EASY ☺	SO-SO 😐	DIFFICULT ☹
Compare body language across cultures	110, 113			
Understand conversations about body language	111, 115			
Use gerunds	112			
Read about how to shake hands	113			
Use infinitives	116			
Use gerunds and infinitives	117			
Read and create a pie chart to express ideas	118			
Write about what body language means in job interviews	119			
Learn about American body language in your community	120			

Past Participles

Past participles are used with the verbs **be** and **get** to show feelings, and as part of the present perfect tense.

For verbs that are regular in the simple past, the past participle is the same as the simple past (verb + **-ed**).

Verb	Regular Simple Past	Past Participle
attend	attended	attended
help	helped	helped
join	joined	joined
marry	married	married
live	lived	lived

For verbs that are not regular in the simple past, the past participle is sometimes the same as the irregular past, but is often spelled or pronounced differently.

Here is a list of some common irregular verbs with their past participles.

Verb	Irregular Simple Past	Past Participle	Verb	Irregular Simple Past	Past Participle
be	was/were	been	leave	left	left
become	became	become	lend	lent	lent
begin	began	begun	lose	lost	lost
break	broke	broken	make	made	made
bring	brought	brought	meet	met	met
build	built	built	pay	paid	paid
buy	bought	bought	put	put	put
catch	caught	caught	read	read	read
choose	chose	chosen	ride	rode	ridden
come	came	come	ring	rang	rung
cost	cost	cost	run	ran	run
do	did	done	say	said	said
draw	drew	drawn	see	saw	seen
drink	drank	drunk	sell	sold	sold
drive	drove	driven	send	sent	sent
eat	ate	eaten	shake	shook	shaken
fall	fell	fallen	shut	shut	shut
feed	fed	fed	sing	sang	sung
feel	felt	felt	sit	sat	sat
fight	fought	fought	sleep	slept	slept
fly	flew	flown	speak	spoke	spoken
forget	forgot	forgotten	spend	spent	spent
get	got	gotten	steal	stole	stolen
give	gave	given	swim	swam	swum
go	went	gone	take	took	taken
grow	grew	grown	teach	taught	taught
hang	hung	hung	tell	told	told
hear	heard	heard	think	thought	thought
hit	hit	hit	throw	threw	thrown
hold	held	held	understand	understood	understood
hurt	hurt	hurt	win	won	won
keep	kept	kept	write	wrote	written
know	knew	known			